EXPERIENCE

LOS ANGELES

⦿ Walking Eye App

YOUR FREE DESTINATION CONTENT AND EBOOK AVAILABLE THROUGH THE WALKING EYE APP

Your guide now includes a free eBook and destination content for your chosen destination, all for the same great price as before. Simply download the Walking Eye App from the App Store or Google Play to access your free eBook and destination content.

HOW THE WALKING EYE APP WORKS

Through the Walking Eye App, you can purchase a range of eBooks and destination content. However, when you buy this book, you can download the corresponding eBook and destination content for free. Just see below in the grey panels where to find your free content and then scan the QR code at the bottom of this page.

Destinations: Download your corresponding essential destination content from here, featuring recommended sights and attractions, restaurants, hotels and an A–Z of practical information, all for free. Other destinations are available for purchase.

Ships: Interested in ship reviews? Find independent reviews of river and ocean ships in this section, all available for purchase.

eBooks: You can download your free accompanying digital version of this guide here. You will also find a whole range of other eBooks, all available for purchase.

Free access to travel-related blog articles about different destinations, updated on a daily basis.

HOW THE DESTINATION CONTENT WORKS

Each destination includes a short introduction, an A–Z of practical information and recommended points of interest, split into 4 different categories:

- Highlights
- Accommodation
- Eating out
- What to do

You can view the location of every point of interest and save it by adding it to your Favourites. In the 'Around Me' section you can view all the points of interest within 5km.

HOW THE EBOOKS WORK

The eBooks are provided in EPUB file format. Please note that you will need an eBook reader installed on your device to open the file. Many devices come with this as standard, but you may still need to install one manually from Google Play.

The eBook content is identical to the content in the printed guide.

HOW TO DOWNLOAD THE WALKING EYE APP

1. Download the Walking Eye App from the App Store or Google Play.
2. Open the app and select the scanning function from the main menu.
3. Scan the QR code on this page – you will then be asked a security question to verify ownership of the book.
4. Once this has been verified, you will see your eBook and destination content in the purchased ebook and destination sections, where you will be able to download them.

Other destination apps and eBooks are available for purchase separately or are free with the purchase of the Insight Guide book.

CONTENTS

LOS ANGELES
OVERVIEW

'Life is good in Los Angeles, it's paradise on Earth!'
From *LA Confidential*

Spanish missionaries named it 'The Angels' and when the sun sets in the early evening and the whole sky looks like it's on fire, it could easily seem like an act of the Almighty. Los Angeles is well known for its Mediterranean climate, ethnic diversity, and sprawling metropolis. In fact, the first thing you'll realise is just how big this city is. It's not big like New York: instead it spreads outward, rather than upward, which makes perfect sense when you remember that this city is prone to the occasional earthquake. Only very recently have the few tiny pockets of skyscrapers been joined by new high-rise builds as advances are made in construction technology and new materials.

The second thing you'll notice is how important having a car is. As the frontier inched westward over a century ago, the rest of America was already evolving and by the time the city was being considered, the automobile was believed to be the way of the future. Recent developments have improved public transportation, but your own wheels make a big difference to ease of travel.

And of course, being the home of Hollywood means that movies play a big part in the history of this West Coast city. Wherever you go, you are likely to encounter locations familiar from the big or small screen, or reminders of the city's many stars.

Los Angeles is a city that many never fully appreciate, but that's simply because they haven't seen the very best it can offer. There are beautiful beaches on one side and breathtaking mountains on the other, the sun shines almost every single day, and the people here are friendly and welcoming to visitors. In recent years, the city has also experienced a cultural renaissance, as creatives of all sorts have rediscovered the pleasures of being based here.

Without a doubt, Los Angeles offers a unique experience; come with an open mind and open eyes and be prepared to be seduced.

IN THE MOOD FOR...

...FINE DINING

If price is no object, then Los Angeles is heaven for the food lover. And even if you have a budget, this city offers an almost infinite number of amazing culinary experiences. Share the restaurant with one or two celebs over brunch at the **Ivy** in Beverly Hills (see page 119), or hit **Ruth's Chris Steak House** (see page 123) for arguably the best steak in Los Angeles – this one won't break the bank. You could head to the **Chateau Marmont Hotel** (see page 88) for afternoon tea, before eating at the Hollywood hotspot, **BOA Steakhouse** on Sunset Boulevard (see page 86), a sophisticated restaurant that offers tempting poultry dishes and superb seafood, plus an extensive cocktail menu and an award-winning wine list. For something a little different, explore **Koreatown** (see page 61) or **Chinatown** (see page 66), where some of the restaurants are open 24/7. However, you'll be spoiled for choice on **Abbot Kinney** in Venice (see page 45), a street almost entirely dedicated to bars and restaurants. Finally, call as far in advance as you can and book a table at **Nobu** in Malibu (see page 38).

...MOVIE INSPIRATION

Los Angeles is the home of TV and movie production and while many big and small screen offerings are now made in studios from Toronto to London, Los Angeles still offers the history and nostalgia of the industry from its very origins. Check out the **Music Box Steps** in Silver Lake (see page 134) that feature in the Laurel and Hardy short of the same name; stand in the footprints of movie legends at the **TCL Chinese Theatre** (see page 84); find your favorite celebrity's star on the **Hollywood Walk of Fame** (see page 85); or visit some of the locations used in classic movies like *Reservoir Dogs* (see page 140), *Pretty Woman* (see page 118), or *Get Shorty* (see page 81). For inspiration before you write your award-winning screenplay, look out over Los Angeles from the iconic **Stahl House** (see page 90), sit on the **beach in Santa Monica** (see page 28) and watch the waves roll in, or hike up to the **Hollywood sign** (see page 142).

...LIVING LUXURIOUSLY

Beverly Hills is the place to head if personal attention is what you seek. Whether you're treating yourself to a mani/pedi, a soothing massage, or a rejuvenating body therapy treatment, **Tomoko Spa** is a world-class center offering the very best in pampering services (see page 125). Alternatively, spend an afternoon living the high life by **shopping on Rodeo Drive** (see page 118), then reward your taste buds at the **Cheese Store of Beverly Hills** (see page 126), a gourmet foods store known for its selection of 500 to 600 cheeses, wines, and other delicacies, including the rarest of all caviars, Golden Imperial Osetra. Then head over to the **£10 bar at the Montage Beverly Hills hotel** (see page 124) and permit yourself to be waited on by the extremely attentive staff as you spend all the money you have in the world.

...MUSICAL MOMENTS

In addition to being the home of the movie industry, Los Angeles is also a mecca for musicians and base for much of the rock and pop music industry. Discover the legacy of all kinds of music at the **GRAMMY Museum** (see page 72) or catch a show at the **Walt Disney Concert Hall** (see page 64). If you want to take advantage of the LA weather, check out the **Hollywood Bowl** (see page 93) for live shows outdoors under the stars, or head inside and get down and dirty to the sound of up-and-coming bands at the legendary **Viper Room** (see page 89) on Sunset Boulevard. Inspired by *La La Land* to seek out the city's jazz scene? Head to the **Rendition Room** (see page 112) in Studio City. Or step back in time at the World War II-era **Rhythm Room LA** (see page 74).

...ROMANCE

Not only will you fall in love with your partner in this city of stars, but you'll fall in love with Los Angeles. Watching the sun set from **Griffith Observatory** (see page 136) is a beautiful experience and a must-do whoever you are with. There are many miles of beach to stroll along with your shoes off. Try **Hermosa and Manhattan** (see page 150) in the south, or walk along the beach from **Venice** (see page 46) to **Santa Monica** (see page 28). Cruise along atmospheric **Mulholland Drive** (see page 128) or **Sunset Boulevard** (see page 80). Finally, have dinner at the **Wilshire** on the stunning two-tier outdoor patio (see page 33) and gaze out over the ocean – be sure to book in advance.

...FAMILY FUN

Keep the whole family happy with a trip to **Universal Studios Park** (see page 102). After they've been on the Harry Potter rides, The Walking Dead attraction, Fast & Furious – Supercharged, the Jurassic Park ride, and much more, you can indulge in lunch or dinner from Krusty Burger to Luigi's Pizza, or even Mel's Diner, from *American Graffiti* (1973). If they still have energy after that, wow them at **Disneyland** (see page 159) – and keep an eye out for Star Wars Land, opening in 2019. Tap into film and TV fandom at the **Warner Brothers Studios** (see page 104), where highlights include the Prop Department – home to more than 450,000 registered artifacts, from *Casablanca* (1942) to *The Hangover* (2009) in arguably the largest prop department in the world. Alternatively, take everyone to a ball game. The Los Angeles Dodgers play at **Dodger Stadium** (see page 138) near Silver Lake and the Angels of Anaheim play at **Angel Stadium** in Orange County (see page 156).

...GREAT ART

See the permanent installations and exhibits from visiting artists at the **Los Angeles County Museum of Art** (see page 83). Among the museum's strengths are its holdings of Asian art; Latin American art, ranging from pre-Columbian masterpieces to works by leading modern and contemporary artists; and Islamic art, of which LACMA hosts one of the most significant collections in the world. In addition, pay a visit to the **Getty Villa** (see page 32) where there are roughly 1,200 artifacts on display at any one time, dated between 6,500 BC and 500 AD, and organized under such themes as Gods and Goddesses and Stories of the Trojan War. Or head to the **Getty Center** for art and architecture with a side order of great views (see page 94). And don't forget to check out the hipster **Downtown Arts District** (see page 62), home to galleries galore.

...ESCAPING THE CROWDS

Avoiding the crowds at many of the attractions in Los Angeles is, in essence, down to timing. Theme parks like **Universal Studios Park** (see page 102) and **Disneyland** (see page 159) will obviously not be as busy during school time as they will be during vacation time, and in general, most places won't be as busy during the week as they would be at weekends or even public holidays. **Santa Monica Beach** (see page 28) draws a bigger crowd than **Venice Beach** (see page 46) if you want some solitude while you're sunning yourself. And spend some time hiking the **Santa Monica Mountains** (see page 30) on a weekday and you'll probably not meet another soul.

...BEING ACTIVE

Outdoor activity is a big element of day-to-day life in Los Angeles. Grab a mountain bike and hit the trails in the **Santa Monica Mountains** (see page 30). You can also take a different kind of bike ride along the **Chandler Bikeway** through Burbank and NoHo (see page 110). If you feel like getting wet, try **scuba diving** (see page 54), learn to surf in **Orange County** (see page 160), or explore the hidden and hard-to-find beaches of **Malibu and Point Dume** (see page 35).

...STREET LIFE

Nothing in Los Angeles is ordinary, but once you soak up some culture and put it all in context you'll definitely get a better understanding of how it fits together and why. Wandering the streets of **Downtown** (see page 75) will offer the chance to see much of historic LA, but it isn't a typical example of Los Angeles street life. That probably comes from **Santa Monica** (see page 29) and the hours that can easily be spent wandering its clean and well cared-for streets. Stroll along the **Ocean Front Walk** (see page 48) all the way to Venice and soak up the endearing insanity on offer there, before exploring the **canals** (see page 52). Or explore charming, offbeat **Eagle Rock** for a glimpse at an up-and-coming, hip neighborhood (see page 140).

...ARCHITECTURE

Don't be fooled by the naysayers – LA has a lot of culture, and not just in the movie industry. As such, there are some stunning buildings dotted about the city, from the iconic **Capitol Records Building** (see page 82), designed to resemble a stack of records, complete with 90-foot rooftop spire, to the modernist masterpiece, the **Stahl House** (see page 90), set in the Hollywood Hills. The interior of the **Bradbury building** (see page 75) in Downtown is a sight that has to be seen to be believed. And so is the **Walt Disney Concert Hall** (see page 64), a breathtaking building designed by Frank Gehry, 'deconstructivist' in style.

...A NIGHT ON THE TOWN

Not even New York is truly a 24-hour town, contrary to popular belief, but **Koreatown** (see page 61) is. This small neighborhood is home to a variety of high-end eats as well as offerings more suitable for a budget. And the nightlife here goes on all night. If you love karaoke, this is the place to go. But Los Angeles' nightlife is legendary, whether you want to catch live music at the **Viper Room** (see page 89), comedy at the **Laugh Factory** (see page 96), or sup classic cocktails at the **Rhythm Room LA** (see page 74). And don't forget to get your tiki on at the vintage **Tonga Hut** in North Hollywood (see page 113)!

...HISTORY

Los Angeles is dripping in history, especially if you're a fan of the movies. You can explore many of the **locations** used in your favorite movies (see page 106) or take a tour: **Downtown LA Walking Tours** offer a number of different themed tours, including 'Downtown Architecture', 'Film & TV Locations', 'Arts District', and 'LA's Beginnings' (see page 70), or take **Philip Mershon's Felix in Hollywood tour** (see page 87). Alternatively, learn about the region's past at the **Natural History Museum of Los Angeles County** – the largest natural and historical museum in the western United States; its collections include nearly 35 million specimens and artifacts and cover 4.5 billion years of history (see page 69). And don't forget to see where the city all started, at the **El Pueblo de Los Ángeles Historical Monument** (see page 73).

...SOMETHING DIFFERENT

If you know your Gemini from your geospace and your ISS from your ionosphere, the **Jet Propulsion Laboratory** (see page 144) is an absolute must– if you can get a ticket. You'll see inside one of the most significant scientific installations that has contributed to almost every single flight into space in some way. Los Angeles actually has many ties to the space program and pride of place is the **Space Shuttle** *Endeavour*, which is on display at the California Science Center (see page 65).

For a truly unusual shopping experience, visit **Nick Metropolis Collectible Furniture Market** in Hollywood (see page 91). And to relax, seek out an almost-invisible operation called **Float Lab Technologies** (see page 49), one of only a handful of companies in the Los Angeles area that offer a 'sensory deprivation experience', in essence, floating in a high-saline solution kept at body temperature, inside a sealed tank with no light and no sound penetrating whatsoever.

NEIGHBORHOODS

Los Angeles covers a vast area and neighborhoods are in fact more like mini-cities in their own rights, with distinctive personalities and attractions. Traveling by car is the easiest way to get between them, despite the risk of traffic.

Santa Monica and Malibu. Perched on the coast, these are two of the most well known cities of Los Angeles. Santa Monica offers a proper pier, a shopping promenade, lots of great bars and restaurants, and arguably the best and biggest beach in the area. Upscale Malibu is more residential, with many gorgeous houses taking advantage of the setting and its beaches and best restaurants tucked away.

Venice. Taking inspiration from its Italian namesake, there is a small network of man-made canals here, but the area is best known for being the epicentre of the weird and wonderful in Los Angeles. Here you'll find the most attractions within a walkable distance, from the restaurant-rich Abbot Kinney to a multitude of shops and bars, to the countless street performers and artists that can be found lining the Ocean Front Walk.

Downtown and around. Essentially the central business district of Los Angeles, this is where the city's pocket of skyscrapers is found. Within this and the surrounding area are little districts like Koreatown and Chinatown, many museums, and major sites like the Los Angeles Memorial Coliseum and Walt Disney Concert Hall.

Hollywood. Everyone on the planet has heard of Hollywood and it's a surprisingly big area. South of the Hollywood Hills you'll find super-trendy West Hollywood, Sunset Boulevard, and mega-tourist attractions like the TCL Chinese Theatre and Hollywood Walk of Fame. This is the epicenter of many quintessential LA experiences.

North Hollywood and the San Fernando Valley. On the other side of the Hollywood Hills and Santa Monica Mountains is the sprawling San Fernando Valley. In addition to being largely residential, it's also where the movie industry is based due to the sheer amount of space. Between Studio City and Burbank you will find Universal Studios, Warner Brothers' Studios, and quirky attractions from tiki bars to an arts district.

Beverly Hills. Second only to Bel Air, Beverly Hills is home to the very rich and this is where to play at living the high life. Strut down legendary Rodeo Drive, explore fashionable Melrose, and eat at the favorite restaurants of many celebrities. Open-top buses run regular tours around stars' homes here, in this district where luxury and celebrity famously intersect.

Los Feliz and Silver Lake. This is a particularly hip area, popular with a bohemian crowd and blessed with an abundance of record stores and coffee shops. This is also an area for top-notch views: hike through Griffith Park to the amazing Griffith Observatory or head up to the legendary Hollywood sign. And don't forget to catch a game at the impressive Dodger Stadium.

Long Beach and Orange County. Long Beach is an underappre-ciated gem and offers several worthwhile reasons to visit, from great seafood to an iconic ocean liner. Driving further south, you come to Orange County, home to Disneyland and beaches from Huntington to Laguna Beach, where you can learn to surf, go whale-watching, and discover the local communities.

SANTA MONICA AND MALIBU

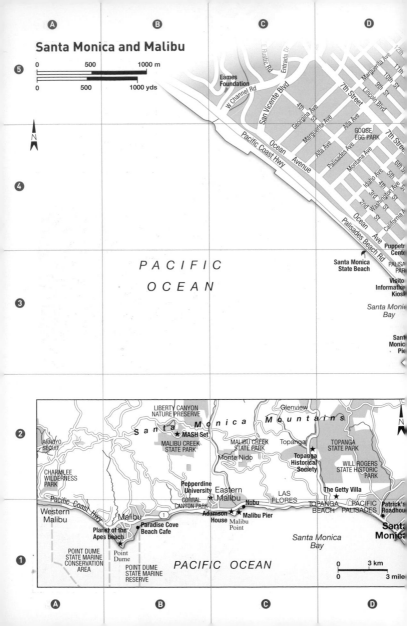

Santa Monica and Malibu

0   500   1000 m
0   500   1000 yds

A **B** **C** **D**

5

N

4

PACIFIC OCEAN

3

Eames Foundation

W Channel Rd

San Vicente Blvd

Entrada Dr

E Rustic Rd

4th

Georgina Ave

Marguerita Ave

7th Street

Alta Ave

12th

Marguerita Ave

11th St

10th St

9th St

Lincoln Blvd

GOOSE EGG PARK

7th Street

Montana Ave

6th St

5th

Idaho Ave

4th

3rd

2nd

Washington Ave

St

California A

Pacific Coast Hwy

Ocean Avenue

Ocean Ave

Palisades Beach Rd

Puppetr Cente

PALISA PAR

Santa Monica State Beach

Visito Informatio Kiosk

Santa Monic Bay

Sant Monic Pie

PACIFIC OCEAN

2

N

LIBERTY CANYON NATURE PRESERVE

Glenview

S a n t a M o n i c a M o u n t a i n s

ARROYO SEQUIT

★ MASH Set

MALIBU CREEK STATE PARK

Monte Nido

MALIBU CREEK STATE PARK

Topanga

TOPANGA STATE PARK

CHARMLEE WILDERNESS PARK

Topanga Historical Society ★

WILL ROGERS STATE HISTORIC PARK

Pepperdine University Eastern Malibu

LAS FLORES

The Getty Villa ★

Pacific Coast Hwy

CORRAL CANYON PARK

Nobu

TOPANGA BEACH

PACIFIC PALISADES

Patrick's Roadhou

Western Malibu

Malibu

Adamson House

Malibu Pier

Santa Monic

1

Planet of the Apes beach ★

Paradise Cove Beach Cafe

Malibu Point

Santa Monica Bay

Point Dume

POINT DUME STATE MARINE CONSERVATION AREA

POINT DUME STATE MARINE RESERVE

PACIFIC OCEAN

0   3 km
0   3 mile

A **B** **C** **D**

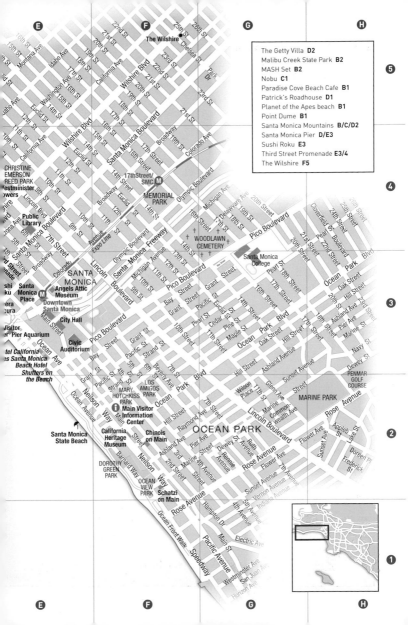

The Getty Villa **D2**
Malibu Creek State Park **B2**
MASH Set **B2**
Nobu **C1**
Paradise Cove Beach Cafe **B1**
Patrick's Roadhouse **D1**
Planet of the Apes beach **B1**
Point Dume **B1**
Santa Monica Mountains **B/C/D2**
Santa Monica Pier **D/E3**
Sushi Roku **E3**
Third Street Promenade **E3/4**
The Wilshire **F5**

Relax on the vast Santa Monica beach, go for a swim, and explore the pier

Without a doubt, **Santa Monica beach** gets a bit more crowded than the likes of Venice beach (see page 46) and way more so than Hermosa and Manhattan Beach (see page 150). This is for a very simple reason: the surrounding area is much more geared to visiting families, with downtown Santa Monica just a short walk away and the pier offering lots of attractions to keep children – and their parents – amused for hours.

As recently as the 1980s, this whole area was pretty far from a tourist attraction, with more drug addicts on the beaches than sun addicts, and the pier in a considerable state of disrepair. However, a massive effort was made to clean up the beaches, repair and rebuild the pier, and revitalize the tourism industry of Santa Monica. Now there are fairground rides, restaurants, shops, and even a video and pinball arcade. **Santa Monica Pier** itself is over 100

years old and has featured in many movies. Tony Stark does a flyby in *Iron Man* (2008) and it features prominently at the end of *Falling Down* (1993), to name just a couple of its appearances. There's also a **Bubba Gump Shrimp** restaurant here, inspired by the movie *Forest Gump* (1994). It won't be the best seafood you've ever eaten, being a little like Kentucky Fried Chicken for shrimp, but it's worth having something just for the novelty.

So the story goes, EC Segar – the creator of Popeye – took inspiration for his famous character from retired fisherman Olaf Olsen, who frequently visited the Pier. Segar captured his best assets: barrel chest, bulging biceps, merchant sailor's peaked cap, a pipe (which he smoked upside down in the rain), and a personality that was as salty as the waters he sailed.

The location of the original Muscle Beach – the actual one where Arnold Schwarzenegger used to work out in the 70s – is on the Ocean Front Walk, just 328ft (100 metres) south of the pier. There's a plaque there now to mark the history, as it's now moved to Venice Beach (see page 46).

Santa Monica Pier; tel: 310-458-8900; http://santamonica.com; map D/E3

Indulge in some retail therapy and be entertained on the Third Street Promenade

In the heart of downtown Santa Monica is the **Third Street Promenade**, an open-air, car-free retail extrvaganza, buzzing with the excitement of lively street performers, cultural activities including outdoor movie screenings, and with such close proximity to the beach that you can still feel the sea breeze.

There's no shortage of shopping opportunities in Santa Monica, all in a walkable area, which feels perhaps more European than American. Check out brands from Abercrombie to Apple and Nordstrom to Nike, alongside independent businesses such as family-owned toy store Puzzle Zoo and rare bookseller Kenneth Karmiole.

It's also a haven for food lovers. Whether you're looking for breakfast, brunch, or pre-movie dining, the promenade is filled with a diverse array of gastronomic options to suit all palates, from morning through to night. For rooftop dining with amazing views of the city, mountains, and the Pacific Ocean, head to **Santa Monica Place** at the south end of the promenade, a shopping mall with a range of dining outlets. And you don't have to break the bank to eat well. All restaurants focus on organic, locally sourced foods. For locally grown produce to purchase yourself, visit the twice-weekly **farmers' market**, open Saturdays and Wednesdays, featuring over two-dozen certified organic farm vendors.

You won't go short of entertainment, either. Among the many vibrant venues are two iconic, newly renovated movie theatres and the **Promenade Playhouse** (www.promenadeplayhouse.com) for theater and comedy, while for an ample supply of free entertainment, the promenade itself becomes an open-air theatre every day thanks to the street artists and performers.

There's plenty of parking, but probably the best spot is one of the multi-level car parks on 4th Street between Wilshire and Broadway.

Third Street Promenade; map E3/4

Hike or bike one of the many trails through the Santa Monica Mountains

Outdoor activity is a big element of day-to-day life in Los Angeles and the whole of the west coast of the US, with the famed dedication to healthy living. And despite the sense of LA as a sprawling city, the presence of the **Santa Monica Mountains** (map B/C/D2), Pacific Ocean, and rugged spaces like Griffith Park (see page 136) mean that the natural world is in fact highly present here. With legendarily good weather and miles of trails and beaches to utilize, it's no surprise that Angelenos are so willing to throw themselves into an outdoorsy lifestyle.

Mountain biking was invented in Marin County, northern California. The bikes we know today were designed and developed over time from off-road riders throwing themselves around the trails found just a couple of miles north of downtown Santa Monica. If you take off-road riding seriously, you'll know it's a very personal thing: your bike is tailored to your needs and you know how it handles. It's extremely unlikely that any bike rental shop in Santa Monica is going to offer high-end bikes with clip-in pedals and bike shoes with cleats, since relatively few people would ask for these. So if you are

dedicated to the sport, you may wish to bring your own bike over. Trans-Atlantic airlines consider a bike to be sports equipment, and while one sports bag used to be free with some airlines, double check this before you travel as more and more have begun charging, often the same for a bike as for a snowboard (if you're thinking of timing a visit to Los Angeles to coincide with a trip to Mammoth Mountain in central California, near Yosemite).

However, this of course doesn't mean you can't just drive into the mountains, park the car and go for a hike. There are over 100 different trails, each one different in length and elevation, thanks to the Santa Monica Mountains covering a very large area. You can even hike to the old set where they filmed both the movie and TV series *M*A*S*H* (1970). While the medic tents have been removed, the location is still recognizable and **Malibu Creek State Park** (www.malibucreek statepark.org; map B2) has gone above and beyond to create a rich experience for hikers. The set is located along Crags Road, the main hiking trail through the park. It's 4.75-miles (7.6km) round trip with a mere 200ft (61 meters) of elevation gain between the parking area at the park entrance and the old set. The hike can be extended to 5.7 miles (9km) by entering the park via South Grassland Trail, or abbreviated to 3.6 miles (5.8km) by entering on Cistern Trail.

Learn about the arts and cultures of ancient Greece, Rome, and Etruria at the Getty Villa

While both are great places to visit, don't get the **Getty Villa** confused with the Getty Center (the latter is near Brentwood, see page 94.) In 1974, oil magnate Jean Paul Getty opened a museum to showcase his art collection in a faux villa in Malibu, based on the remains of the Villa dei Papiri in Herculaneum. The 1966 Guinness Book of Records named Getty as the world's richest private citizen, worth an estimated $1.2 billion (approximately $9 billion in 2017). Following his death, the museum inherited $661 million and in 1997, the artifacts and paintings were moved to the Getty Center, while the villa was converted into a museum for Getty's collection of Mediterranean antiquities, reopening in 2006. Architects Jorge Silvetti and Rodolfo Machado had worked magic on semi-restoring the building while also transforming it.

There are around 1,200 artifacts on display at any one time, dating from between 6,500 BC and 500 AD. These are organized under a number of themes, such as Gods and Goddesses or Stories of the Trojan War. For a great overview, start your visit in the Timescape room, where a display maps the different civilizations along with information on the art they created.

With so many interesting exhibits, it is quite possible to lose a few hours exploring the galleries. Classical civilization buffs will especially enjoy the Greek gods collection of various items including statuary and delicate, painted jars, while everyday items like ancient coins and jewelry bring the periods to life. Changing special exhibitions and interactive exhibits keep it fresh for repeat visitors.

Be aware that you need to book a timed ticket to visit the museum, as walk-ins are not accepted. Entrance is free and ideally, you'd book a ticket for early in the morning in order to beat the hoards. Always book well in advance at peak times.

Getty Villa; 17985 Pacific Coast Highway; tel: 310-440-7300; www.getty.edu/visit/villa; map D2

Enjoy a romantic dinner and Californian Cabernet Sauvignon at the Wilshire

Wedged in-between Chelsea Avenue and 25th Street is the **Wilshire**, a deceptively simple neighborhood restaurant with an organic, farmers' market-led approach to constructing their New American cuisine, which draws on various local and international influences and presents dishes in a mouthwatering and simple style. The décor in the bar area is elegant, with banks of candles and moody lighting, a theme that continues through to the main patio dining room, where fire pits and multitudes of tea lights continue to wash guests in soft lighting.

This is a place serious about food and with the focus on seasonal ingredients, it's not the cheapest restaurant in Santa Monica, but it's not the most expensive either. There's also a Happy Hour exclusively at the front bar offering snacks, small plates, and pizette, from $7–$16, and $9 specialty cocktails and $6 wine and beer, from Mon–Sat, 5–7pm.

Despite the stunning interior, eating outside on the equally striking two-tier patio is the real draw. The wide variety of entrées include lobster and shrimp risotto – with Parmesan, lemon, herbs, truffle, and shellfish sauce – scallops, branzino fillet, horseradish-pistachio crusted salmon, line-caught ling cod, chicken breast, duck breast, BBQ pork chop...and so on. Add a Cabernet Sauvignon from northern California and you've got yourself an amazing dining experience. It's actually quite a romantic restaurant, with intimate dining soft lighting. The very helpful, knowledgeable, and friendly staff will happily open your wine at the table and then leave you in peace as you gaze across the table into the eyes of your loved one.

The Wilshire; 2454 Wilshire Boulevard; tel· 310-586-1707; http://wilshirerestaurant. com; map F5

Conclude your day of exploring Santa Monica with an evening at Sushi Roku

Sushi Roku is a high-end restaurant, but what makes it really appealing is its location, and the fact that you can sit at the bar, order whatever you want, when you want, and slowly sup sake at the same time, all the while making conversation with the bar staff. Perfect after a day spent exploring the area on foot. Located on the corner of Santa Monica Boulevard and Ocean Avenue – metres away from both the beach and the heart of the Third Street Promenade – you can practically feel the energy coming off of Santa Monica as you sit and relax.

If you've spent the day exploring, with maybe a little shopping (see page 29) or hiking through the mountains (see page 30), or just a day spent on the beach, now it's time to wind down. The food on offer here is excellent and reasonably priced, and there's also a very respectable selection of sake, at least equally as important. There's also the all-American Happy Hour where 'bites' cost from $3 to $10 and include Wagyu sliders, albacore tacos, sushi rolls, and fried calamari. Liquid refreshment like hot saki, sangria, or a Roku Fusion Martini costs just $5–10.

If you're looking for a traditional, hushed sushi spot, this isn't the place for you. Sushi Roku was one of the first ultra-modern Japanese restaurants in Los Angeles, with the décor and music to boot. But for fine food in a lively atmosphere, you can't go wrong. Try the incredible sushi and sashimi, which are always top-notch, while the French-Japanese fusion dishes hit the spot. Sample dishes include spicy tuna on crispy rice and seared albacore sashimi in garlic ponzu.

There's valet parking on Ocean Avenue, $10 with validation for the first 3 hours, between 11am–11.30pm; the garage closes at midnight.

Sushi Roku; 1401 Ocean Avenue; tel: 310-458-4771; map E3

Seek out the hidden beaches of Malibu and Point Dume

The coastal city of **Malibu** is not really laid out in the traditional sense of having a downtown area and surrounding suburbs. Instead, it follows the coastline along the **Pacific Coast Highway** and much of it can't be seen from that road. It's also quite a residential area and an exclusive one at that. Malibu Colony Road, which is just south of the PCH, is essentially billionaires' row. Seventy-five or so properties sit on a private beach – not one of them costs under $10 million. Many movie and music stars have properties here, including Jason Statham, Tom Hanks, and Lee Majors.

Around the Point Dume peninsula, a few more miles up the PCH, there are a number of hidden away roads that are deliberately hard to find. Broad Beach Road is one such place, and Pierce Brosnan, Robert Redford, and Danny DeVito have properties along here. After many years of wrangles over access, you'll find that most of the beaches are accessible to the public, but not all. Many of Malibu's wealthy, celebrity homeowners are keen to preserve their privacy, and do so with private security and some more creative tactics.

Point Dume (map B1) itself is pretty awesome, and Big Dume

Beach is accessible to the public. The PCH strays away from the coast for a little bit and within this peninsula is a maze of roads with some very big and very expensive houses. David Letterman has a property here, as do Martin Sheen, Barbra Streisand, and Sean Penn.

You can head down, park and swim from the beach – you'll almost always find a few surfers here – and if you feel adventurous, you can spend an hour or so clambering over rocks, a cliff top, and vegetation to reach a small beach called Pirate's Cove to the west. This is where Charlton Heston falls to his knees in the infamous final shot of the *Planet of the Apes* (1968).

By the way, Latigo Beach – where it is said ex-presidents surf in *Point Break* (1991) – is fictional, so don't waste your time driving up and down the PCH for hours trying to find it, like many others have.

35

Cruise the PCH, explore Pacific Palisades, and grab lunch at Patrick's Roadhouse

The iconic **Pacific Coast Highway**, famed for hugging California's coast, appears in this area as a fast-moving four-lane road that whisks between Malibu and Santa Monica. Malibu sits either side of the PCH, with the Santa Monica Mountains on one side and Pacific Ocean on the other. But between Malibu and Santa Monica is an area that sits just in from the coast and stretches west to east, rather than south to north like Malibu – this is **Pacific Palisades**. It's a gorgeous, green, mostly residential area that is also home to many movie stars – Tom Hanks likes it so much he currently has three properties here. Sunset Boulevard (see page 80) goes right through it on its way to the PCH, and at the end of Sunset Boulevard is a collection of normal shops, like a grocery store, bank, post office, gas station, and other day-to-day necessities.

Pacific Palisades is elevated on a hillside, so the views are across the ocean, rather than actually having the water wash up to your front door. If you drive a few minutes along the PCH towards Santa Monica you might catch a glimpse of a odd-looking, green and white building on the left as you approach the lights to turn left into Entrada Drive. This is **Patrick's Roadhouse**, a locally-beloved, retro American diner that

looks like some sort of monument to Ireland. It even gets a mention in *Point Break* (1991) "He goes to Tower Records, buys some CDs, has lunch at Patrick's Roadhouse..."

Famed for decades thanks to its friendly ambiance, charismatic owners, and popularity with local celebrities, Patrick's remains a much-loved spot. The most famous regular customer must be Arnold Schwarzenegger, who even has a dish named for him – the 'Governator,' an Austrian breakfast dish composed of eggs, sausage, peppers, and potatoes, which was originally crafted for the Terminator by his mother. Schwarzenegger also donated a special iron chair to the restaurant, which guests are free to sit in! Nevertheless, this isn't your regular celebrity hangout – it's far too down-to-earth for that. It can be noisy, it's inexpensive, and it's somewhat off the beaten track unless you are driving between Santa Monica and Malibu. But this is a gem, with quintessential diner fare – a lot to chose from – and it's all good. If you fancy lunch or even dinner instead though, note that it's BYO. There's plenty of parking out front.

Patrick's Roadhouse; 106 Entrada Drive; tel: 310-459-4544; http://patricksroad house.info; map D1

Dine with the stars at the famous Nobu restaurant

Not only is Robert De Niro a talented actor, but he's also a successful businessman, co-owner of three hotels and the **Nobu** restaurant chain. The original outlet of this evergreen hotspot is in New York, but by far the most well-known is the location in Malibu. Popular with locals, tourists, and celebrities alike, it is not at all uncommon to see a movie star enjoying a spot of lunch here.

And the reason is obvious. The view is amazing and the food is exquisite. In fact, it's so close to the beach, you can see the footprints. The restaurant's minimalist aesthetic – wood paneling, no white table cloths – creates an understated feel that complements its environment; likewise, the menu is as stellar as its surroundings. The menu is traditional Japanese and Peruvian fusion and be aware, it isn't cheap. For a table with a great view, you will need to book and you might want to think of booking this as far in advance as you possibly can.

The name comes from Japanese celebrity chef, Nobuyuki 'Nobu' Matsuhisa. He had opened restaurants in Japan, Peru, and even Alaska, before finally opening one in Los Angeles near where The Ivy is now (see page 119). It became a favorite with celebrities, he met Robert De Niro and the rest is history. His signature dish is black cod in miso, although the sweet glaze it comes in can be quite overwhelming if you don't have a sweet tooth.

If you do see a star, the best protocol – and the coolest – is to leave them alone. After all, they want to enjoy their food as well and chances there will be at least a few photographers outside waiting for them.

Nobu Malibu; 22706 Pacific Coast Highway; tel: 310-317-9140; http://nobu restaurants.com; map C1

Discover Paradise Cove, a hidden-away restaurant off the Pacific Coast Highway

The **Paradise Cove Beach Cafe** is down a side road called Paradise Cove Road, that you'll easily miss, off the PCH. However, if you were to try and get in here on a bank holiday weekend, say Memorial Day in May or Labor Day in August, the queue of waiting cars spilling out onto the PCH, causing all manor of hold ups, would certainly alert you to the eatery's location.

It's an odd mix of tat and taste and arguably even a little overpriced, but the reason you're there is to soak up the sun, marvel at the view, and relax on this secluded patch of sand, with a fancy cocktail in your hand. Guests are more than welcome to go and lie out on the sand after their meal and many take advantage of the opportunity, so feel free to pack a couple of beach towels and a sun umbrella in your car before you go. You can order just about any seafood dish you like here, from grilled slabs of fresh ahi tuna to the outlandish Iced Seafood Tower, a looming plate of whole Maine lobster, crabs, jumbo shrimp, salmon, scallops, prawns, and more. There's also burgers, pork ribs, pasta, prime steak...you name it. Anything generally considered 'American,' plus a pretty good selection of draft beer, wine, and cocktails.

Just remember to always have a designated driver. The LAPD and California Highway Patrol have a zero tolerance policy on DUI. The sizeable parking lot offers dramatically subsidized parking costs if you spend over $20 at the cafe, so it's worth coming here with a plan to eat.

Paradise Cove Beach Café; 28128 Pacific Coast Highway; tel: 310-457-2503; www.paradisecovemalibu.com; map B1

VENICE

Venice

0 ___ 500 ___ 1000 m
0 ___ 500 ___ 1000 yds

N

Santa Monica Bay

PACIFIC OCEAN

Cedar St
Pine St
Maple St
Ocean Park Blvd
Oak St
Hill St
Ashland Ave
Pier 70
Sunset Ave
Lincoln Boulevard
7th St
6th St
Beverley Ave
5th St
Hill St
Ashland Ave
Glenn Ave
Dewey
4th St
5th St
7th St
LOS AMIGOS PARK
3rd St
2nd St
Pier Ave
Marine St
Dewey Ave
Waren Ave
Rose Avenue
MARINE PARK
Nelson Way
California Heritage Museum
Main St
Hill St
3rd St
Pier Ave
Navy St
OCEAN PARK
Whole Foods Market
Sunset Ave
Vernon Ave
Lincc
OCEAN VIEW PARK
Enterprise Fish Co
Marine St
Cerveteca Latin American Restaurant
La Cabaña Restaurant
The Bicycle Whisperer
Waren Ave
Rose Avenue
5th St
Sunset Avenue
Vernon Avenue
Indiana Avenue
Indiana Ct
Broadway St
The Firehouse
Rose Cafe
Hampton Dr
4th St
OAKWOOD
California
Venice Ale House
Pacific Ave
Main Dr
Brooks Ave
Hal's Bar & Grill
Blue Bottle Coffee
St Clara Ave
Salt & Straw
The Brig
Palms
Ocean Front Walk
Float Lab Technologies
Main St
Abbot Kinney Blvd
Kreation Juicery
Abbot's Pizza Company
Shima
Venice Beach
Kinney Plaza
i
Abbot Kinney Memorial Branch Library
Jay's Rentals
Pacific Ave
Muscle Beach
Ride Venice
Speedway
N Venice Blvd
S Venice Blvd
Venice Canals
Dell Ave
Hinano Cafe
South Bay Trc
Venice Fishing Pier
Ocean Front Walk
Speedway

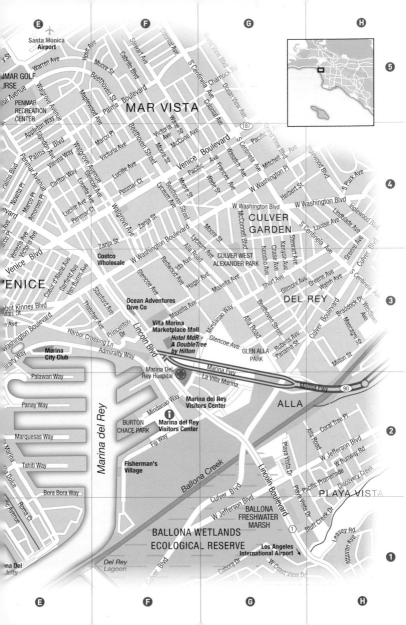

Hit Rose Avenue for dinner at the Firehouse on a summer's evening

More of less marking the beginning of Venice, **Rose Avenue** (map C4–E5) has been called the new Abbot Kinney (see page 45) and while it still has a long way to go before it offers any real competition, it does have some good restaurants worth popping into. Along the 0.8 mile (1.3km) stretch between Main Street and Lincoln Boulevard there are a number of coffee shops, snack bars, and restaurants that are always packed out, both through the day and in the evening. While it isn't actually pedestrianized, multiple traffic light crossings and one dedicated pedestrian crossing make it a good place to be on foot, although it can get a little frustrating if you're driving along here.

At the far end, by Lincoln Boulevard is **La Cabaña** (738 Rose Avenue; tel: 310-392-7973; http://lacabana venice.com; map D4), which does proper Mexican food. **Cerveteca Latin American Restaurant** (523 Rose Avenue; tel: 310-310-8937; http://cervetecala.com; map C4) is a pretty laid-back hangout for burgers and Latin comfort foods, while further down towards the beach, the **Rose Cafe** (220 Rose Avenue; tel: 310-399-0711; http://rosecafevenice.com; map C4) is an iconic Venice hangout, serving up Southern Californian takes on American classics, plus bakery options. Just across the street, however, the **Firehouse** (213 Rose Avenue; tel: 310-396-68; http://firehousevenice.com; map C4) is a highly recommended favorite. This all-day Californian-American diner-style eatery is built into an old actual firehouse, so the doors swing open and you can watch the world go by.

The only thing that might alarm you is a very peculiar 'Ballerina Clown' art installation that sits atop the main entrance to the CVS pharmacy directly opposite the Firehouse. But that aside, this is a great place to eat before wandering down Main Street and trying a few bars later in the evening. It does get busy, especially in the summer and there's always a good atmosphere.

Choose from the outrageous amount of restaurants that line Abbot Kinney

Just a few minutes walk from the beach, **Abbot Kinney** is a mile-long boulevard that is legendary in Southern California. Essentially, every other building is a bar or restaurant, and each and every one is amazing. Added to which, on the first Friday of every month, **food trucks** line the road and fill the car park from 5pm in the afternoon. It's a rarity to have so much choice of really great food in such a small area. Quite often, the trucks will follow a different theme for a month; in May for example, it's Cinco de Mayo, so many of the food trucks will serve Mexican. Tacos, burritos, tortas, sopes, tostadas, mulitas, quesadillas, and more.

Then there are the restaurants. You could go for health conscious Japanese sushi made only with brown rice at **Shima** (1432 Abbot Kinney Boulevard; tel: 310-314-0882; map D3) or **Hal's Bar & Grill** (1025 Abbot Kinney Boulevard; tel: 310-396-3105; www.halsbarandgrill.com; map D3) for distinctive, seasonal American cuisine in a spacious, casual setting, surrounded by world-class contemporary art, or maybe something from the finest pizzeria in Venice, **Abbot's Pizza Company** (1407 Abbot Kinney Boulevard; tel: 310-396-73340; www.abbotspizzaco.com; map D3).

It doesn't have to just be dinner. Kick back and kill some time at **Blue Bottle Coffee** (1103 Abbot Kinney Boulevard; tel: 510-653-3394; https://bluebottlecoffee.com; map D3) or maybe a healthy refreshment at **Kreation Kafe and Juicery** (1202 Abbot Kinney Boulevard; tel: 310-314-7778; www.kreationjuice.com; map D3), or if it's hot and sunny maybe a home-made ice cream sundae is in order from **Salt & Straw** (1357 Abbot Kinney Boulevard 310-310-8483; https://saltandstraw.com; map D3).

The Brig (1515 Abbot Kinney Boulevard; tel: 310-399-7537; www.thebrig.com; map D3) is a great place for a drink after dinner. It's a bustling nightspot with a mid-century modern vibe and live music – but there's plenty of choice.

http://abbotkinneyboulevard.com; map C3–E3

Relax on the vast Venice beach, go for a swim, or take a surf lesson

People don't always realise just how big **Venice beach** is until they look out over the wide stretch of sand. From the Ocean Front Walk (see page 48) to the actual water's edge it's a good 985ft (300 metres). But as you explore the beach heading northward towards Santa Monica, you'll see that the space is well-used: sometimes for permanent volleyball courts laid out in the sand, or for yoga classes, surfing classes, and of course, lifeguard huts.

Most people, however, usually make their camp on the beach closer to the water's edge, especially since the sand can get quite hot during the summer (beware walking barefoot). The closer to Santa Monica Pier you get, the more crowded the beach will be.

Surfers tend to hang out on the south side of a little rocky outcrop that's in line with 17th Street, in between the skate park and Muscle Beach. **Learn to Surf** (http://learntosurfhb.com) is a surf school that has outlets in Huntington Beach and Newport Beach (see page 154) as well as Santa Monica (see page 28) and here. The **Kapowui Surf School** (http://kapowuisurfclub.com) is another that comes highly recommended.

Prices vary depending on how long you want the lesson for, your level of competency, and whether you need to hire the wetsuit and board as well. The website has all the information you need to work out exactly how much you can expect to pay, depending on what you want to get out of it.

Los Angeles usually gets its rain from January to March and you'll notice after a lot of rain, no one goes in the water, even if there are good waves. Sadly, the water can be quite dirty from the drain run off

from the streets, so the locals will wait a day or so.

Should you fancy a late night stroll on the beach, to walk off dinner perhaps, be warned: chances are you'll have a LAPD helicopter spotlight in your face before long and a cop shouting through a loudspeaker telling you to get off the beach. There is a long-standing, midnight-to-5am curfew on Los Angeles beaches, partly to do with public safety – they have no way of knowing you're not going to run into the water and get swept away by a riptide, all in the black of night – and partly to deter rough sleepers.

Note that parking will be a little tricky around here. There is a public pay parking lot opposite 601 Ocean Front Walk, or, depending on how confident you feel, you could try and find a spot along the narrow, one-way road called Speedway that runs parallel to Ocean Front Walk, just behind it.

Venice Beach; http://venicebeach.com; map C3–D3

Get your freak on and discover the Ocean Front Walk

Ocean Front Walk (map C4–E1) is divided into two sections, the Santa Monica end and the Venice end, but by far the most popular bit starts at Navy Street and goes all the way along to Venice Pier. At weekends during the summer you can hardly move, yet somehow people on rollerblades and skateboards will miraculously be able to weave in between these heaving crowds without knocking anyone over. Most of the time. Not only are there many bars and restaurants along this stretch, but this is where you will see a proliferation of street

aselling trinkets, t-shirts, tat, and beach towels.

Muscle Beach (map C3), the outdoor gym made famous by Arnold Schwarzenegger, is now permanently based along here – it's original location was in Santa Monica. Be sure to check out this living reminder of the origins of the American fitness boom.

Many of the buildings here have huge murals painted on the side and you can also see the famous massive 100 x 21-ft (30.5 x 6.4-meter) painting parodying Botticelli's iconic *Birth of Venus*. Originally painted in 1980 by Rip Cronk, in this incarnation, Venus is replaced with a beachside roller-skating woman. It's at 25 Windward Avenue.

As you take a gentle stroll along the Ocean Front Walk, it's not un-common to see street performers juggling chainsaws, somersaulting through the air, riding unicycles, or playing live music. You'll see a wealth of home-made art on sale and all manner of weird and won-derful hand-painted bits and piec-es. This pedestrian pathway is one of the main attractions in Venice and from here, many of the most interesting things to see and places to go are only a short walk away.

Immerse yourself in darkness and remove all eternal stimuli with a float tank experience

Tucked away, just off the Ocean Front Walk at the busy end of Venice Beach, near Brooks Avenue, is an almost-invisible operation run by a man with aging rock star looks who goes by the name Crash. Called **Float Lab Technologies**, it's one of only a handful of companies in the Los Angeles area that offer a 'sensory deprivation experience,' which is in essence, floating in a high-saline solution kept at body temperature, inside a sealed tank with no light and no sound penetrating whatsoever. Purged of external stimulation, you can enjoy the most relaxed and meditative state imaginable. The dissolution of all mental distraction means your mind is free to fly among infinite inter-dimensional otherworlds.

A solution of epsom salt is used to increase water density, causing the body to float with the face above the water, like lying in the Dead Sea. When your arms float to the side, sensitivity is greatly reduced because the air and water within the tank are the same temperature as your skin, and the feeling of any body boundary disappears. Each session costs $40 and lasts two hours.

When the big isolation tank craze hit a few decades ago, it was said that some famed artists came up with their best ideas inside the tanks and that the mind invented vivid colors and patterns. For the first 40 minutes it's possible to experience itching in various parts of the body – a phenomenon also reported to be common during the early stages of meditation. The last 20 minutes often end with a transition from beta or alpha brainwaves to theta, which typically occurs briefly before sleep and again at waking. In a float tank, the theta state can last indefinitely without the subject losing consciousness. Many use the extended theta state as a tool for enhanced creativity and problem solving or for super learning. The more often the tank is used, the longer the theta period apparently becomes.

Float Lab Technologies; Ocean Front Walk; tel: 310-396-3336; https://floatlab.com 801; map C3

Watch the world walk past from the comfort of the Venice Ale House

The **Venice Ale House** is always popular and at weekends it's heaving, which means if you can get in, there's a great atmosphere to be enjoyed. As the name suggests, their primary focus is on beer and the Venice Ale House prides itself on having a selection that's chosen because of its locality and the environmental integrity of the brewery. Almost every choice comes from California: the House Beer is from Santa Monica, the Pilsner is from Davis, California, the Sculpin IPA is a pale ale from San Diego, and so it goes on. Try the Beer Skate – a sampler served on a skateboard, perfect for trying a few brews. Plus they have they have own interpretation of many popular cocktails, a pretty impressive wine list, and even a respectable choice of sake.

The food here is also really good and the American-style menu offers great burgers and a whole host of seafood, plus a ton of salads, and vegan and gluten-free options too, including waffles! This is a real spit-and-sawdust type of joint, so there's no need to dress up. In fact, anything more than jeans and sneakers would probably make you stand out.

This is also a good place to pick your copy of *LA Weekly*, the excellent, free publication that comes out every Thursday. While many of the distribution bins dotted around Los Angeles will be empty an hour after they've been filled, the Venice Ale House usually still has some kicking about a few days later and that's pretty rare. There's outdoor seating too, right on the corner of Rose Avenue and the Ocean Front Walk, so you can hang out and watch the weird and wonderful world of Venice slowly drift past in front of you.

Venice Ale House; 2 Rose Avenue; tel:310-314-8253; http://venicealehouse.com; map C4

Speed freaks

A two-minute walk up Rose Avenue to where it crosses Main Street is where the first bus blew up in the action movie *Speed* (1994), as Keanu Reeves was getting coffee from what is now The Firehouse (see page 44).

50

Get stuck into a well-deserved burger in the no-frills setting of the Hinano Café, then head to the Pier

If you're looking for a genuine Venice dive bar with character to spare, head for **Hinano Cafe**, an uber-casual, beachside hangout, just steps from the Venice pier. It has been serving up great beer and burgers to a diverse crowd since 1969, and was reportedly Jim Morrison's favorite Venice bar. While it doesn't have the range of beers that say, the Venice Ale House does, it's still a great place to grab a casual bite and enjoy a cold one, whether you want to get out of the sun or set yourself up for the evening. A typical dive bar, you will find pool tables, a jukebox, and a range of screens showing football.

Hinano attracts a big crowd in the evenings and at weekends, so it's best to either get there a little early, prop up the bar, and get stuck in, or cruise in later on in the evening after you've been to a few other places beforehand. Since it's near Venice Pier, there's always a crowd at weekends as there are many other cafés and bars nearby. It's not a sports bar by any stretch of the imagination, but if there is a big game on, chances are they'll show it here, although there aren't very many TVs. Note that it's cash only.

Venice Pier more or less marks the end of the quirkiness that Venice offers. Anything further south from here starts to become more residential; the Ocean Front Walk disappears and apartment buildings sit right on the sand. You can still walk down here, but the shops disappear and the craziness is all behind you as the area becomes **Marina Del Rey**.

Hinano Café; 15 W Washington Boulevard; tel: (310) 822-3902; http://hinanocafe venice.com; map D2

Rent a bike and pedal around Venice, before visiting the area's namesake canals

A bike is a great way to explore Venice and even Santa Monica (see page 30), thanks to the pedestrianized areas and wide boardwalks. There are a number of bike rental companies in Venice, but among the best are **The Bicycle Whisperer** (724 Vernon Court; tel: 310-612-1409; map D4), **Ride Venice** (1915 Ocean Front Walk; tel: 310-954-0974; http://ridevenice.com; map C3), and **Jay's Rentals** (1915 Ocean Front Walk; tel: 310-954-0974; map C3). Prices are roughly the same and usually start at about $6 or $7 per bike per hour. Just be sure to get a good lock from wherever you

hire it from and double check what the policy and procedure is if it's stolen, because around Venice, if it's not locked, it will disappear. It is also important because bikes are not allowed along the canals, so you will need to lock it up when you stroll around here.

Venice is called Venice because of the **canals** (map D3), built in 1905 by developer Abbot Kinney as part of his 'Venice of America' plan. Kinney sought to recreate the appearance and feel of Venice, Italy, in Southern California: a cultural Valhalla dedicated to the fine arts, complete with canals, gondolas, and imported Ital-

ian gondoliers. The dramatic plan drew a lot of attention and helped to sell development lots to people enticed by the elegant designs, studded with arched bridges.

However, the rise of the car in the early part of the 20th century resulted in the canals quickly seeming outdated, and in 1929, the bulk of them were filled in to create roads. The canal area was left to disrepair, with muck and silt building up in the remaining canals for decades, although the area was listed on the National Register of Historic Places in 1982. Finally, in 1992, the canal district was renovated: new sidewalks and walls were built and the canals themselves were drained. After reopening in 1993, the neighborhood has never looked back as its become a highly desirable and pricey residential district.

Today, waves of bright flowers tumble over the fences and ducks nestle under upturned boats on tiny jetties. Only a block away, traffic thunders ceaselessly down Pacific Avenue, but here in the wildlife sanctuary formed by the canal system, all is calm. You can pick your way along rutted paths, over humpbacked bridges, and past well-tended gardens, admiring the architecture, the birds, and the flowers.

In recent years, there has been extensive renovation work on many of the old houses, and many large, modern – and expensive – houses have been built, especially since this part of Los Angeles has begun to turn into what's being called 'Silicon Beach' with large tech companies opening up around here and wealthy CEOs buying property. For those lucky enough to reside here, canal-side living offers a uniquely relaxing outdoorsy kind of life. Note the rowboats, kayaks, and canoes moored in front of the houses.

Jump in the water on a scuba diving trip off the coast

Marina Del Ray is home to the world's largest man-made yacht harbor and is the jumping-off point for many sea-faring activities. Head here to plan a **scuba diving** excursion, whether you're a beginner or experienced. It isn't as expensive as you might think. All equipment is provided, as every PADI-certified dive school will have everything you need. **Ocean Adventures Dive Co** is probably the best dive school in the area and whatever your level of experience, there is something here for everyone.

If you've never dived before, you could try either the Pool Experience for $149 or go straight in with the Catalina Ocean Dive Option for $499. The former might be better for anyone feeling nervous, but rest assured, you'll be shown how to use all the gear. With the latter, you'll be diving with three professionals, who will ensure your safety and make sure you thoroughly enjoy the experience. There's also a refresher course for anyone who is PADI-certified, but perhaps hasn't logged any dive time for a little while. That's $149 for a group session or $199 for a private session.

California offers some of the most spectacular recreational diving in the world. Southern California is blessed with a chain of local islands known as the **Channel Islands**, which offer a world-class kelp diving experience. For local divers, Catalina (see page 163), Santa Cruz, and Anacapa are seasonal favorites.

Catalina Island is just a couple of hours away by boat off the Orange County coast and offers year round recreational activities. Its waters are highly protected and offer a spectacular opportunity to experience Southern California diving at its best in a safe environment. The Ocean Adventures Dive Co website has lots of information and a calendar of events and dives taking place – you'll soon discover that diving has its own, very friendly, community.

Ocean Adventures Dive Co; 4144 Lincoln Boulevard; tel: (310) 578-9391; http://ocean adventuresdiveco.com; map F3

Wander up Main Street and have dinner at the Enterprise Fish Co restaurant

Sitting very close to the much-disputed boundary line between Santa Monica and Venice is the **Enterprise Fish Co** restaurant. It doesn't look like much from the outside, but inside it's massive, much bigger than you'd think. The inviting interior features a beautiful brick finish, with hardwood floor and original cast iron ceiling beams, plus there's an outdoor eating area that quickly fills up in the evening. As it's name suggests, this is predominantly a fish restaurant and it prides itself on serving locally-caught, sustainably-sourced fish – the selection is impressive.

Happy Hour here is a big draw. From 4–7pm Mon–Sat, and 8–10pm on Sun, you can get wine or well cocktails for $4; margaritas, mai tais, and bloody Marys for $6; and really good draft beer (Stella Artois, Hefeweizen, Pacifico) for just $4. The food is equally well-priced, with $1.50 oysters, $6 shrimp quesadillas, and steamed clams or mussels for $9.

However, the Jambalaya comes highly recommended: andouille sausage, shrimp, chicken, and jalepeño corn bread, enjoyed sitting outside on an evening in May or June. Gather some friends, order a round of beer and contribute to the warm vibe that this eatery radiates.

After dinner, take a stroll along Barnard Way and walk off dinner, perhaps exploring a bit of **Main Street**, where you can try out some of the bars. At the weekend, there's always a crowd, and during the summer there is a great atmosphere, as many of the bars open their doors and people sit outside. The bars on Main Street aren't like the Hinano Cafe (see page 51) or even the Venice Ale House (see page 50): you probably won't get in wearing flop-flops, a t-shirt, and ripped denim shorts, just FYI.

174 Kinney Street; tel: 310-392-8366; http://enterprisefishco.com; map C4

DOWNTOWN AND AROUND

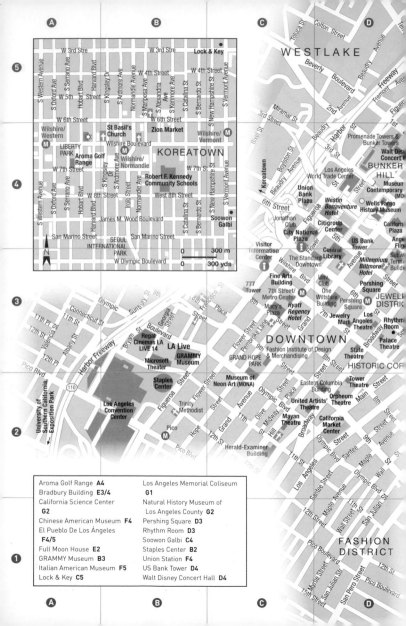

Map Legend

WESTLAKE

KOREATOWN

BUNKER HILL

DOWNTOWN

GRAND HOPE PARK

HISTORIC COR

JEWELRY DISTRICT

FASHION DISTRICT

SEOUL INTERNATIONAL PARK

LIBERTY PARK

W 3rd Stre
Lock & Key
W 4th Street
W 5th Street
W 6th Street
Wilshire Boulevard
St Basil's Church
Zion Market
Wilshire/Western
Aroma Golf Range
Wilshire/Normandie
Robert F. Kennedy Community Schools
West 8th Street
James M. Wood Boulevard
San Marino Street
W Olympic Boulevard
Soowon Galbi
Wilshire/Vermont

Promenade Towers & Bunker Towers
Walt Dis Concert
Los Angeles World Trade Center
Museum Contemporary (MO
Union Bank Plaza
Westin Bonaventure Hotel
Wells Fargo History Museum
Jonathan Club
Citigroup Center
Californ Plaza
City National Plaza
US Bank Tower
Ange Flig
Visitor Information Center
The Standard Downtown
Central Library
Millennium Biltmore Hotel
Subw Term Build
Fine Arts Building
Univ. Club
Pershing Square
777 Tower
7th Street/Metro Center
One Wilshire Building
Pershing Square
JEWELF DISTRIC
Macy's Plaza
Hyatt Regency Hotel
Jewelry Mart
Los Angeles Theatre
Rhythm Room
Fashion Institute of Design & Merchandising
State Theatre
Palace Theatre
Regal Cinemas LA LIVE 14
LA Live
GRAMMY Museum
Microsoft Theater
Museum of Neon Art (MONA)
Eastern Columbia Building
Tower Theatre
Staples Center
United Artists' Theatre
Orpheum Theatre
Los Angeles Convention Center
Trinity Methodist
Mayan Theatre
California Market Center
Herald-Examiner Building

300 m
300 yds

Aroma Golf Range **A4**
Bradbury Building **E3/4**
California Science Center **G2**
Chinese American Museum **F4**
El Pueblo De Los Ángeles **F4/5**
Full Moon House **E2**
GRAMMY Museum **B3**
Italian American Museum **F5**
Lock & Key **C5**

Los Angeles Memorial Coliseum **G1**
Natural History Museum of Los Angeles County **G2**
Pershing Square **D3**
Rhythm Room **D3**
Soowon Galbi **C4**
Staples Center **B2**
Union Station **F4**
US Bank Tower **D4**
Walt Disney Concert Hall **D4**

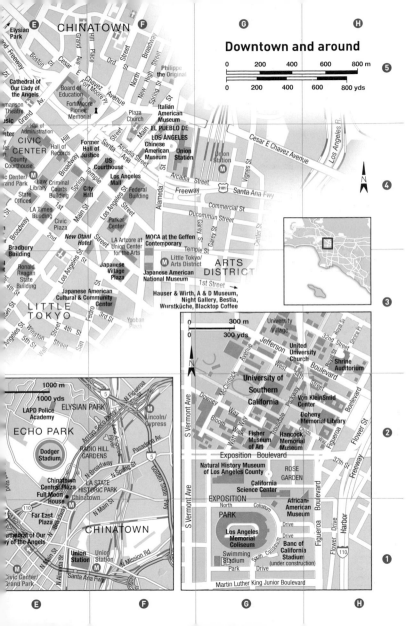

Downtown and around

CHINATOWN

Elysian Park
Cathedral of Our Lady of the Angels
Board of Education
Philippe the Original
Fort Moore Pioneer Memorial
Plaza Church
Italian American Museum
EL PUEBLO DE LOS ANGELES
CIVIC CENTER
Hall of Administration
Hall of Records
Former Hall of Justice
US Courthouse
Chinese American Museum
Union Station
Hall of Justice
County Courthouse
Law Library
Criminal Courts Building
City Hall
Los Angeles Mall
Federal Building
State Offices
LA Times Building
Civic Plaza
Parker Center
New Otani Hotel
LA Artcore at Union Center for the Arts
MOCA at the Geffen Contemporary
Bradbury Building
Ronald Reagan State Building
Japanese Village Plaza
Little Tokyo/Arts District
Japanese American National Museum
ARTS DISTRICT
LITTLE TOKYO
Japanese American Cultural & Community Center
Yaohan Plaza

Hauser & Wirth, A & D Museum, Night Gallery, Bestia, Wurstküche, Blacktop Coffee

University of Southern California
University Village
United University Church
Jefferson
Shrine Auditorium
McClintock Avenue
Von KleinSmid Center
Doheny Memorial Library
Downey Way
Bloom Way
Fisher Museum of Art
Hancock Memorial Museum
Exposition Boulevard
Natural History Museum of Los Angeles County
ROSE GARDEN
EXPOSITION PARK
California Science Center
African-American Museum
Los Angeles Memorial Coliseum
Banc of California Stadium (under construction)
Swimming Stadium
Martin Luther King Junior Boulevard
S Vermont Ave
Figueroa
Flower St
Harbor Freeway
110

ECHO PARK
LAPD Police Academy
ELYSIAN PARK
Lincoln/Cypress
Dodger Stadium
RADIO HILL GARDENS
LA STATE HISTORIC PARK
Chinatown Central Plaza
Full Moon House
Chinatown
Far East Plaza
CHINATOWN
Cathedral of Our Lady of the Angels
Union Station
Civic Center/Grand Park
Santa Ana Fwy
110

Watch the home team, the Los Angeles Kings, in an exciting NHL game at the Staples Center

Arguably the most exciting American sport to watch is NHL, or ice hockey and traditionally, the cities that actually have cold winters, like Chicago and Boston, have good NHL teams. But Los Angeles is an exception. Along with the Anaheim Ducks (see page 155) the **LA Kings** are a pretty exciting team to watch.

Like every team in every sport, they have their good seasons and bad seasons and since they won the Stanley Cup (the big trophy) in 2014, the LA Kings sadly haven't been able to maintain that high standard. However, they have some of the best players currently in the NHL and the **Staples Center**, where they play, is a great venue. And one thing Americans do better than anyone else is make any sporting event a memorable one, even if it's just a regular season game. Everything from huge celebrations when the home team scores, to the Kiss Cam, to freebie giveaways, to the crowd during the intervals, really add up to make it a fun night out.

The Staples Center is a 21,000-capacity, multi-purpose sports arena in Downtown, located next to the **Los Angeles Convention Center** complex along Figueroa Street. It's also where the **LA Lakers** basketball team play. There are multiple parking lots around the Staples Center and additional ones will be opened up on game day, but if you're going to see a game, get there a few hours early and have some dinner at one of Downtown's many great restaurants. Also, be prepared to get stuck in traffic exiting the event and more than likely get lost driving around Downtown – it's a maze. There are some surprisingly rough areas very close by that you don't particularly want to get stranded in, but just try to get back to a road you know, then go from there. Tickets are available from TicketMaster et al.

Staples Center; 1111 S Figueroa; tel: 213-742-7100; www.staplescenter.com, www.nhl.com/kings; map B2

Scratch the surface of the 24-hour lifestyle in Koreatown, from cocktails to golf

Centered near Eighth Street and Western Avenue, **Koreatown** is considered part of the Mid-Wilshire district. In the 1920s and 30s it was very much a swinging spot for Hollywood celebrities, and the location of the Ambassador Hotel, which hosted the Academy Awards in its first couple of decades. More sombrely, this was also the site of Robert F. Kennedy's assassination. Koreatown is known for having one of the largest concentration of nightclubs and entertainment venues in the country, from dive bars to high-end cocktail speakeasies and karaoke clubs, as well as restaurants that are open 24 hours a day.

Soowon Galbi (856 S Vermont Avenue B; tel: 213-365-9292; map C4) is a staple of the Koreatown dining scene. One of the most popular styles of Asian cuisine is Korean barbecue, aka KBBQ or *go-gigui* (literally 'meat and roasting'). Unlike many KBBQ spots, Soowon Galbi is not 'all-you-can-eat,' but the Combo Specials are excellent if you want to order a big plate of different things and share everything.

The entrance to **Lock & Key** (239 S Vermont Avenue; tel: 213-389-5625; http://lockandkey.la; map C5) is a red door that leads to an intriguing wall of doorknobs and keyholes,

where you have to try different ones to get in. Once inside this stylish speakeasy, there's a small selection of beer and wine – but the cocktail list is the reason you're here.

It wouldn't be Koreatown if there wasn't at least one golf course or a driving range nearby. When you want to hit some balls, head to the **Aroma Golf Range** (3680 Wilshire Boulevard; tel: 213-387-2111; http://aromaresort.com; map A4), a 150-yard (137-meter) enclosed driving range in the heart of the district on Wilshire Boulevard. Set across four storeys, it has 15 teeing stations on each floor and an automated ball return system utilizing pneumatic tubes to tee your ball up. Lessons are also available here if you feel your performance isn't up to par.

Gallery-hop your way around the Downtown Arts District

It took two outsiders to fully appreciate the visual potential of Los Angeles: Ed Ruscha from Omaha, Nebraska, and David Hockney from Bradford, UK. Ruscha's homage to the Hollywood film industry depicts the famous sign shifted to the crest of the Santa Monica mountains in Cinemascopic proportions. Meanwhile, Hockney arrived in LA in 1964 and promptly mailed a postcard to his dealer in London: 'I have found the world's most beautiful city, a promised land.' Hockney then did for Los Angeles what Canaletto had done for Venice, becoming its supreme celebrant.

This sprawling metropolis of sparkling lights, beautiful people, and flamboyant architecture, perched on the edge of the desert facing the Pacific Ocean, might be viewed as one enormous art environment. Los Angeles artists took what was at hand in the streets, at the beach, in the factories, and crafted beautiful objects that reflected the mirage that is the City of Angels.

The now-designated **Arts District** in the far east of Downtown is the hub of today's art scene. The area has gradually transformed from a edgy collection of abandoned factory buildings and warehouses into a fashionable hub of live/work lofts and studios, today lined with top-notch restaurants and cafés, stylish boutiques, and of course, an abundance of hot galleries. This historic neighborhood attracts the young and hip, who want to live and hang out in its walkable, gritty-meets-gentrified streets.

The first place to head to is **Hauser & Wirth** (901 E 3rd Street; tel: 213 943 1620; www.hauserwirth losangeles.com). Opened in 2016, this mega-gallery and exhibition space occupies an entire block, housed in historic 19th and early 20th century buildings. Come for the dazzling space, stay for the worthwhile shows, which have so far had a focus on artists with a connection to the LA art scene, such as Paul McCarthy.

From here, the most satisfying thing to do is wander the streets, checking out any galleries which catch your eye. Dozens of new places have opened here in the last few years. Some of the most interesting spots include **A+D Museum** (900 E 4th Street; tel: 213-346-9734; http://aplusd. org), which focuses on promoting awareness of progressive architecture and design; **The Box**

(805 Traction Avenue; tel: 213-625-1747; http://theboxla.com) for a carefully-curated presentation of local and international artists; and the **Night Gallery** (2276 E 16th Street; tel: 323-589-1135; http://nightgallery.ca), the exciting epicenter of LA's youthful, occasionally guerilla art scene.

There is no shortage of great, happening restaurants to try out here, from local favorite, **Bestia** (2121 E 7th Place; tel: 213-514-5724; http://bestiala.com) for super-trendy, rustic Italian grub considered some of the best food in town – you'll need to be on the ball to snare a reservation – to **Wurstküche** (800 E 3rd Street; tel: 213-687-4444; www.wurstkuche. com), an industrial space serving up hearty fare, including great sausages and Belgian-style fries. Or head to **Blacktop Coffee** (826 E 3rd Street) for an excellent brew and light bites.

Arts District; map G3–off map

Catch a concert at the $274-million crown jewel of the LA Music Center, the Walt Disney Concert Hall

Home of **Los Angeles Philharmonic Orchestra** (Los Angeles Philharmonic Orchestra; tel: 323-850-2000; http://laphil.com), the **Walt Disney Concert Hall** is the fourth hall of the Los Angeles Music Center. It opened in 2003 and seats 2,265 people. The unique architectural style by Frank Gehry is known as deconstructivism, and makes for a breathtaking building.

The initial funding came from Lillian Disney, widow of Walt, who made a gift of $50 million in 1987 for a performance venue to the people of Los Angeles. It was in tribute to Walt Disney's long-standing dedication to both the arts and the city. Painstaking attention has been paid to the acoustic design by Minoru Nagata, and as a result it has received much acclaim. The auditorium is configured in a 'vineyard' style, which allows for seating on all four sides of the stage.

The Walt Disney Concert Hall is just one part of the LA Music Center, which is officially called the **Performing Arts Center of Los Angeles County**. One of the largest performing arts centers in the US, over 1.3 million people every year visit the events, arts festivals, outdoor concerts, arts activities, workshops, and educational programs. In addition to classical music, big-name bands sometimes play here and there's even the occasional movie premiere. The events program is listed on the website and this is the best way to check what's on.

Parking is available directly beneath Walt Disney Concert Hall; enter on Second Street or Lower Grand Avenue. There's also a number of all day car parks around the Downtown area.

Walt Disney Concert Hall; 111 South Grand Avenue; http://waltdisneyconcerthall.ticket offices.com; map D4

Indulge your inner geek with a trip to the California Science Center to see the Space Shuttle *Endeavour*

Los Angeles has a surprising number of links to the space program: the Jet Propulsion Laboratory is based in Glendale (see page 144); the Apollo Command modules were built and tested in Downey, where there is a museum nearby, the Columbia Memorial Space Center at 12400 Columbia Way, Downey (tel: 562-231-1200; http://columbiaspace science.org); and the legendary Edwards Air Force Base is just a few hours drive north of Los Angeles.

Pride of place, however, is probably the **Space Shuttle *Endeavour***, which is on display at the **California Science Center**. To get the *Endeavour* here was no easy task. First, it flew into LAX on the back of a specially-fitted 747 after having done a couple of fly-bys over the city. Then it embarked on a very slow, 12-mile (13km), 68-hour journey through the city streets to get to its final destination. Trees along the way had to be temporarily uprooted and telegraph roles moved to get the 86-ton, 78-feet wide orbiter to the Science Center while 1.5 million people lined the sidewalks to watch and cheer.

Along with the *Endeavour* and a permanent display that showcases the amazing history of the Space Shuttle program with one of the external fuel tanks and things like landing gear, there's always a whole host of other exhibitions and displays, plus an IMAX theater, but these will often only be on for a limited time. Check the website to see what's on. Some events might require tickets; general admission is free, but it is encouraged to leave a donation to the upkeep of this special place. Parking is on site.

California Science Center; 700 Exposition Park Drive; tel: 323-724-3623; http://californiasciencecenter.org; map G2

65

See how LA's Chinatown stacks up and sample some authentic Chinese fare

The earliest Chinatowns first appeared in cities on the west coast of the US and were created as communities to help ease the transition into American culture. San Francisco was home to the first in 1848, with Los Angeles following a few years later, spurred by the California Gold Rush and the Transcontinental railroad. However, the original **Chinatown** (http://chinatownla.com) was demolished to make room for Union Station and the Chinese community was encouraged to live in other areas, rather than remain in just one district. A separate commercial centre, colloquially known as 'New Chinatown,' opened for business in 1938.

It might not be the biggest in the US in terms of population (that honor goes to New York), but if you like authentic Chinese food, this is really the only place to go in the city.

Full Moon House (960 N Hill Street; tel: 213-537-0792; http://fullmoonhouserestaurantinla.weebly.com; map E2) is a quality, relaxed eatery with a long menu of traditional family-style Chinese dishes and a focus on seafood. Here, you'll find all that you probably came to Chinatown for in the first place, including Peking duck, Kung Pao chicken, lacquered vegetables, hot pot seafood, and fried pork, all prepared with a level of execution that surpasses much of the area's surrounding competition.

At the turn of the century, business in Chinatown was arguably at its lowest, with many in the community relocating to Monterey Park in LA's suburbs. However, over the last decade, the whole of Downtown Los Angeles has been going through something of a revival, with a lot of new construction and revitalization encouraging industry and business back to the area, and that has certainly spread to Chinatown.

You'll need to park on the street and pay by meter, but it shouldn't be too hard to find a spot.

Watch the returning Rams play at the Los Angeles Memorial Coliseum

Once upon a time, Los Angeles had two prominent teams, the LA Raiders and the **Rams**. But the NFL is a funny thing. As an official organisation, it rarely creates new teams and instead, cities around the US can bid for existing teams, offering deals and stadiums. Consequently, teams relocate, which does little for fan loyalty. In fact, before they played in Los Angeles, the Raiders were based in Oakland, while the Rams are from St Louis.

Since the 1980s, the Raiders have moved back to Oakland and are now about to move to Las Vegas, and the Rams returned to St Louis but are now back in Los Angeles. But, regardless of if you follow a particular team or the city instead, it does mean that you can now enjoy an American Football game in Los Angeles, which is a quintessential American experience.

Until their new stadium is completed, the Rams will play at **the Los Angeles Memorial Coliseum** (3911 S Figueroa Street; tel: 213-747-7111; http://acoliseum.com; map G1), an open-air, natural grass stadium with 93,000 capacity.

Meanwhile, the **Chargers**, who played in LA for one year in 1960, following their formation, are moving back to Los Angeles from San

Diego. The Chargers currently play in the **StubHub Center** (18400 Avalon Boulevard) the primary tenant of which is the LA Galaxy soccer team. They will use this stadium from 2017 until they move into **Los Angeles Stadium at Hollywood Park**, along with the Rams, currently scheduled to be open in time for the 2020 NFL season. As LA will be hosting the Olympic Games in 2028, great efforts are being made to improve existing sports facilities and build even more.

Tickets for Rams and Chargers games are available through Ticketmaster, StubHub and all the usual suspects, as well as through the team's websites. The best seats to get are as close to the 50 yard line as possible, but they'll probably cost a little more.

www.therams.com; www.chargers.com

Relax in Pershing Square Park, one of LA's most quintessential public spaces

While only one square block in size, **Pershing Square Park** is a perfect place to sit, soak up a little sun, and maybe have a spot of lunch while you're exploring Downtown. Bordered by 5th Street to the north, 6th Street to the south, Hill Street to the east, and Olive Street to the west, it's a perfect place to look upon the much improved area that surrounds the public park. The Downtown area of Los Angeles is, in essence, the central business district, although LA is so big there are several distinct CBDs, like Culver City, Century City, Santa Monica, and so on. However, this area has a surprising amount of history, with buildings like the Bradbury Building (see page 75) and City Hall. A considerable effort is being made to build new luxury apartment towers and generally clean up the area.

In 1992, the park was closed for a major $14.5-million two-year redesign and renovation. It now features a concert stage, a seasonal ice rink, and small plazas with seating, plus hosts a variety of community events. It also serves as a major location for television shows, films, and private parties. The **Pershing Square Downtown Stage** is a six-week summer concert series with free music, films, and events four days a week.

At the southern end of the square is an abstract structure, created by Ricardo Legorreta, containing a fountain. It is intended as a representation of Los Angeles' agricultural history, with the bell tower, aqueduct, and orange spheres symbolising water flow from California's mountains to citrus farmers' groves.

Pershing Square; 32 S Olive Street; tel: 213-847-4970; www.laparks.org/ pershingsquare; map D3

Learn about the region's past at the Natural History Museum of Los Angeles County

The largest natural history museum in the western United States, the **Natural History Museum of Los Angeles County** boasts collections that feature nearly 35 million specimens and artifacts and span 4.5 billion years of history.

There are both permanent exhibitions and temporary ones that change over time. Don't miss the permanent installation, Becoming Los Angeles, which tells the 500-year story about how Southern California went from tiny pueblo to sprawling metropolis: from the Spanish Mission era through the Mexican Rancho era and the early American Period, beyond the emergence of a new American city in the late 19th and early 20th centuries, and the Great Depression to World War II and the present day.

Age of Mammals is another must-see. This tells an epic evolutionary story that spans 65 million years and has a unique focus, being the first permanent museum exhibit to explore the evolution of mammals – from the end of the dinosaur era to the rise of humans – within the context of epochal changes in the Earth's geology and climate.

If dinosaurs are your thing, you're in luck: the NHMLA has

many many fossils, specimens, interactive features, displays, and a 14,000-square-foot Dinosaur Hall that rivals the world's leading museums with skeletons of a stegosaurus, triceratops, and a tyrannosaurus rex.

On top of the admission fee, you can pay extra for additional features – usually the special exhibitions that are only there for a limited time. Parking is available in the Museum's parking lot on Exposition Boulevard and Bill Robertson Lane.

Natural History Museum of Los Angeles County, 900 Exposition Boulevard; tel: 213-763-3466; https://nhm.org/site; map G2

Benefit from local knowledge and take a guided tour of Downtown

There are a number of different ways to explore Downtown Los Angeles. You could plan a tour of your own and wander about at your own leisure or you could take advantage of the knowledge of a local. There are a number of tours to chose from, should you decide to take the latter approach, but one of the better ones is run by **Downtown LA Walking Tours**, who offer a number of different themed tours, including 'Downtown Architecture,' 'Film & TV Locations,' 'Arts District,' and 'LA's Beginnings.' Tours are structured so that tourists visiting the city and even locals who have lived in LA for years can enjoy it. The aim is that each guest comes away having learnt something new.

One favorite is the 'Haunted Tales Tour.' 'Be prepared to hear about the dark side of Downtown LA with this haunted tales tour of murders, mysteries and unresolved crimes,' as the website says. Highlights include hearing about the Chinatown massacre of 1871, the *LA Times* bombing in 1910, the Black Dahlia murder, and the haunting of Pio Pico. Although note that this particular one also carries a parental guidance notice due to the nature of the stories and graphics shown during the tour.

Another favorite is the 'Old and New Downtown LA.' On this one, you'll see Angels Flight – the shortest railway in the world, Grand Central Market, and St Vincent's Court in the Jewelry District.

Tours take place throughout the day and each one lasts about two hours, so wear comfortable shoes. It costs $17 per person, but children 12 and under can go along for free. Alternatively a private, individually tailored tour can be arranged with Downtown LA Walking Tours' founder, a long-time, local Los Angelino by the name of Neel. Each tour has a different starting point, so check the website in advance so you can find a place to park.

Downtown LA Walking Tours; tel: 213-399-3820; http://dtlawalkingtours.com

Imagine you've made your way west, like the trailblazers of old, at Union Station

Equally as iconic as Manhattan's Grand Central, **Union Station** represented the end of the line for many when they made their way west, having first arrived in the US by boat at an east coast port like New York. Completed in 1939, it was designed by John and Donald Parkinson, who are also responsible for Los Angeles City Hall. Los Angeles almost had an elevated train system like New York City or Chicago, but instead it was decided in 1926 to build a terminus and consolidate different railroad lines. Votes were cast by Los Angeles locals, but their opinion was heavily swayed by the *Los Angeles Times*, a lead opponent of elevated railways. So instead, Union Station was built where the original Chinatown (see page 66) had stood – a result of the xenophobia that was rife at the

time. Today, Chinatown is a block or two north of Union Station. The station was designated as a Los Angeles Historic–Cultural Monument 1972 and placed on the National Register of Historic Places in 1980.

There are some interesting things to see and do here, enough to happily fill an afternoon. There are a number of coffee shops, salad bars, and even an ice cream parlor. Plus the all-important 'art and architecture tour' that covers the historic Union Station and spaces not generally open to the public, including the Historic Ticketing Hall. However, these only run once a month, usually on the second Sunday of each month, for about two hours in length.

Union Station; 800 North Alameda Street; http://unionstationla.com; map F4

Film set

Union Station has been used in countless movies over the years from *Blade Runner* (1982), where it served as the open-plan police station, to *The Dark Knight Rises* (2012) as the 'courtroom' where the Scarecrow sentences 'guilty' Gothamites. It's also appeared in *Predator 2* (1990), *Catch Me If You Can* (2002), and *Hail, Caesar!* (2016).

Dig deep into the history of music at the GRAMMY Museum

The **GRAMMY Museum®** opened in 2008 to celebrate the GRAMMY Awards'® 50th anniversary. For music buffs and casual fans alike, the museum is a one-stop shop for appreciation of the music awards, the artistry involved with creating great music, and the technical side of the recording process. The intent is to educate and inspire on the subject of American music, its history, and its legacy, drawing on the long-standing traditions as well as innovations.

It consists of four floors offering historical music artifact displays, interactive instrument stations, recording booths, and a 200-seat theater. The Museum starts on the top floor and guides you downstairs as you move through the exhibits. Check out handwritten song lyrics; costumes worn by GRAMMY Award®-winning artists such as Michael Jackson, Daft Punk, Alicia Keys, and Gwen Stefani; exhibits explaining various musical genres, with the ability to listen to seminal songs; and an interactive experience where you can learn about producing tracks in soundproof booths, including recording your own.

The 30,000 sq ft (2,787 sq m) Museum regularly updates and changes exhibits, so it's always worth checking the website to see what's on. Past exhibits have included a *Michael Jackson show; Say it Loud: The Genius of James Brown*, and *The Taylor Swift Experience*. In addition, the Museum frequently holds live performances, seminars, classes, and discussions in its theater. It costs $13 for adults and is open daily. All in all, it's probably wise to set aside about three hours to see everything. There are quite a few convenient parking sites dotted throughout downtown.

The GRAMMY Museum; 800 W Olympic Boulevard; tel: 213-765-6800; www.grammymuseum.org; map B3

See where the City of Angels was established at the El Pueblo de Los Ángeles Historical Monument

This tiny district is centered around the old plaza, where the city of Los Angeles was established in 1781, first as a farming community under Spanish rule (1781–1821), then Mexican (1821–1847), and finally American (after 1847) through most of the 19th century. The **El Pueblo de Los Ángeles Historical Monument** has an authentic, Spanish-style feel and the area is comprised of 26 historical structures, 11 of which are open to the public, as well as the famous Olvera street, which is full of local, independent vendors selling a range of goods. The whole area was listed on the National Register of Historic Places in 1972.

There are many historical sights to see, including **Olvera Street**, which was converted by local merchants in 1930 into the colorful Mexican marketplace that remains today; the **Avila Adobe**, which was built in 1818 and is the oldest surviving residence in Los Angeles; the **Old Plaza Firehouse**, the oldest firehouse in Los Angeles; and the **Pelanconi House**. Built in the 1850s, it's the oldest surviving brick house in Los Angeles. Four of the many buildings have been restored as museums and archaeological excavations in the Pueblo have uncovered artifacts dating all the way back to the first days of settlement.

Also located here is the **Chinese American Museum** and the **Italian American Museum** and in addition to the permanent attractions, many events are held here, from a weekend-long celebration of the Cinco de Mayo in May to the Los Angeles birthday celebration in August and Mexican Independence Day.

El Pueblo de Los Ángeles; 125 Paseo De La Plaza; tel: 213-628-1274; http://elpueblo. lacity.org; map F4/5
Chinese American Museum; 425 N. Los Angeles Street; tel: 213-485-8567; http://camla.org; map F4
Italian American Museum; 644 North Main Street; tel: 213-485-8432; http://italianhall. org; map F5

Step back into World War II-era Los Angeles at the Rhythm Room LA classic cocktail bar

Union Station) gave it its current form in 1925.

For decades, the Rhythm Room was an classic cocktail bar attracting people from all walks of life, until the decline of the Hayward Hotel, which housed the bar. Following a period of neglect, it closed in the 1970s and stayed that way until summer 2017, when new owners sought to bring this quintessential speakeasy back to life. Today, the Rhythm Room LA's underground lounge is back in action. With no natural light, the vibe is all about low-lit, cozy ambiance, with mid-century-style décor rubbing up against industrial chic – see the bare brick walls, inviting leather furniture, and exposed beams.

The aim of the owners is to capture that cocktail-supping, the-hell-with-it 1940s spirit, juxtaposed with a space that makes people want to stay put. So witness the many games on offer from pool to chess to foosball to ping pong – there is no shortage of entertainment on hand. In addition, frequent performances of live jazz and other musical acts are helping this old-time bar swing again.

American soldiers on leave during World War II might easily have stayed at the Hayward Hotel in Downtown Los Angeles and perhaps descended the marble stairs into the hotel's basement club, the **Rhythm Room LA**, for a shot straight up and some live music. The club, which was founded in the 1920s, was one of the attractions of the hotel at the corner of Sixth and Spring streets in the city's financial district. It was one of the city's first high-rise buildings when it went up in 1905, and architects John and Donald Parkinson (City Hall and

Rhythm Room LA; 206 W 6th Street; www.rhythmroomla.com; map D3

Stroll around Downtown and spot locations from many, many movies and TV shows

So much of Los Angeles has been filmed and photographed from different angles to make it look like somewhere totally different and Downtown is no exception. The Michael Mann epic *Heat* (1995) utilises many locations, especially around Downtown, from the security truck robbery near the beginning of the movie on. Another great location from the same movie and also *Fight Club* (1999) is the foyer of the Citigroup Center at 444 S Flower Street, where there's a permanent installation by Michael Heizer called 'North, East, South, West,' consisting of four seemingly simple stainless steel geometric forms, which echo the spirit of Imperial Roman architecture.

Another must-see if you're a movie fan is the **Bradbury Building** at 304 S Broadway (map E3/4). It may not look like much from the outside, but once you step inside you'll instantly recognise it as 'that building' from *Blade Runner* (1982). The unique structure features a Victorian centre court with wrought-iron stairs and birdcage elevators. It was constructed in 1893 after being commissioned by gold-mining millionaire Lewis L. Bradbury and is listed as a National Historic Landmark. It's still in use today as a working retail/commercial space so you'll need to go on a tour to see the inside. For more information, or to see available tours, check out http://laconservancy.org. You can also call 213-623-2489 for more information.

The Pacific Electric Building at 6th & Main was used as police headquarters in *Se7en* (1995) and all of Downtown was used to create the Unnamed US City that the movie was set in. Much of critically-adored *Mad Men* was filmed around Downtown, while the Convention Center (1201 S. Figueroa Street) was used recently in HBO's *Westworld* series. **Los Angeles City Hall** is another easy-to-recognise building and has featured in *LA Confidential* (1997) among other movies.

HOLLYWOOD

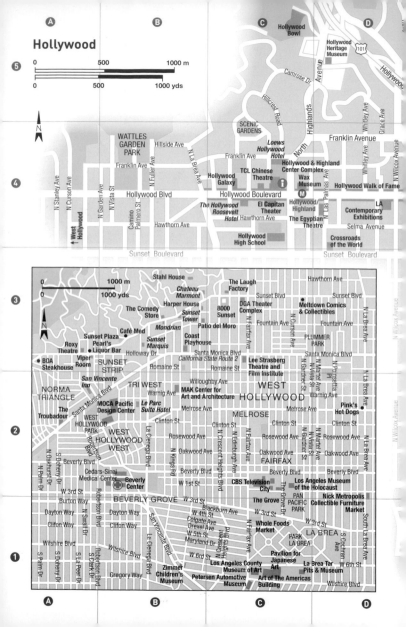

Hollywood

A · B · C · D

5

0 — 500 — 1000 m
0 — 500 — 1000 yds

N

Hollywood Bowl
Hollywood Heritage Museum
101
Hollywood

Camrose Dr
Hillcrest Road
Highlands
North
Whitley Ave
Grace Ave

SCENIC GARDENS
Loews Hollywood Hotel
Franklin Avenue

WATTLES GARDEN PARK
Hillside Ave
Franklin Ave
N La Brea Ave
N Fuller Ave

4

Franklin Ave
N Vista St
Camino Palmero St
N Garden St

Hollywood Galaxy
TCL Chinese Theatre
Hollywood & Highland Center Complex
Wax Museum
Las Palmas Ave
Hollywood Walk of Fame

N Stanley Ave
N Curson Ave

Hollywood Blvd
Hollywood Boulevard
Hollywood Boulevard
i
M
Hollywood/ Highland
LA Contemporary Exhibitions

The Hollywood Roosevelt Hotel
El Capitan Theater
Hawthorn Ave
The Egyptian Theatre
Selma Avenue

← West Hollywood
Hawthorn Ave
Hollywood High School
Crossroads of the World

Sunset Boulevard
Sunset Boulevard

---

0 — 1000 m
0 — 1000 yds
N

3

Stahl House
The Laugh Factory
Hawthorn Ave

Chateau Marmont
Sunset Blvd
Sunset Blvd

Harper House
The Comedy Store
8000 Sunset
DGA Theater Complex
Meltdown Comics & Collectibles
N La Brea Ave

Sunset Tower
Fountain Ave
Fountain Ave
N Curson Ave

Café Med
Mondrian
Patio del Moro
PLUMMER PARK

Sunset Plaza
Pearl's
Roxy Theatre
Liquor Bar
Sunset Marquis
Coast Playhouse
Santa Monica Blvd
California State Route 2
Santa Monica Blvd

Viper Room
SUNSET STRIP
Holloway Dr
Romaine St
Romaine St
Lee Strasberg Theatre and Film Institute

BOA Steakhouse
San Vincente Inn
Warnig Ave
Willoughby Ave

NORMA TRIANGLE
TRI WEST
MAK Center for Art and Architecture
WEST HOLLYWOOD
Warnig Ave
N Martel Ave
N Poinsettia Pl
N Gardner St

Santa Monica Blvd
MOCA Pacific Design Center
Le Parc Suite Hotel
Melrose Ave
MELROSE
Melrose Ave
Pink's Hot Dogs

The Troubadour
WEST HOLLYWOOD PARK
Clinton St
Clinton St
Clinton St
N Edinburgh Ave
N Fairfax Ave
N Vista St

2

WEST HOLLYWOOD WEST
La Cienega Blvd
Rosewood Ave
Rosewood Ave
Rosewood Ave
N Gardner St

N Oakhurst Dr
N Kings Rd
Oakwood Ave
Oakwood Ave
Oakwood Ave
FAIRFAX
N La Brea Ave

S Doheny Dr
N Palm Dr
Robertson Blvd
Beverly Blvd
Beverly Blvd
Beverly Blvd
Beverly Blvd

Cedars-Sinai Medical Center
Beverly Center
CBS Television City
Los Angeles Museum of the Holocaust
PAN PACIFIC PARK

BEVERLY GROVE
W 3rd St
Blackburn Ave
The Grove Dr
The Grove
Nick Metropolis Collectible Furniture Market

Burton Way
Dayton Way
W 4th St
Colgate Ave
Orexel Ave
N Crescent Heights Blvd
N Fairfax Ave

Dayton Way
Clifton Way
W 5th St
Maryland Dr
Whole Foods Market
PARK LA BREA
S Cochran Ave
South La Brea Ave

1

Clifton Way
N Swall Dr
S Clark Dr

Wilshire Blvd
Le Cienega Blvd
W 6th St
LA BREA

S Peer Dr
S Doheny Dr
S La Peer Dr

Gregory Way
Zimmer Children's Museum
Petersen Automotive Museum
Los Angeles County Museum of Art
Pavilion for Japanese Art
Art of The Americas Building
La Brea Tar Pits & Museum
Wilshire Blvd
W 6th St

S Palm Dr

A · B · C · D

N Wilcox Avenue
N Wilcox Avenue

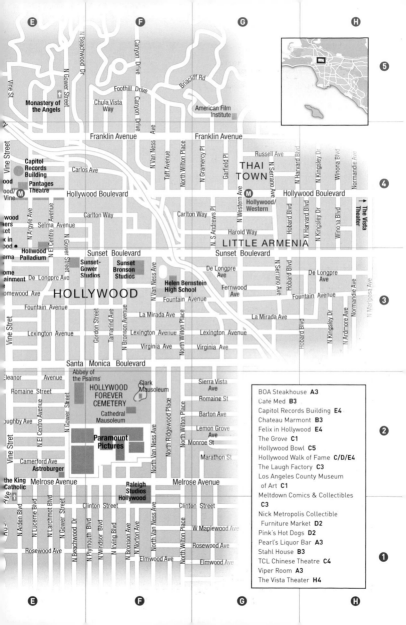

E   **F**   **G**   **H**

N Beachwood Dr

N Gower Street

Vine St

Canyon Drive

Foothill Drive

Chula Vista Way

Canyon Drive

Briarcliff Rd

American Film Institute

5

Monastery of the Angels

Vine Street

Franklin Avenue   Franklin Avenue

Capitol Records Building

Carlos Ave

N Van Ness Ave

Taft Avenue

North Wilton Place

N Gramercy Pl

Garfield Pl

Russell Ave

THAI TOWN

N Serrano Ave

N Harvard Blvd

N Kingsley Dr

Winona Blvd

Normandie Ave

4

ood

ood/
Vine

M

Pantages Theatre

Hollywood Boulevard

M

Hollywood/
Western

Hollywood Boulevard

N Western Ave

Hobard Blvd

N Harvard Blvd

N Kingsley Dr

Winona Blvd

The Vista Theater

wood
ters
eet
k in
ood

N Argyle Ave

N El Centro Avenue

N Gower Street

Carlton Way

Selma Avenue

Carlton Way

N S Andrews Pl

Harold Way

LITTLE ARMENIA

ama
Hollwood
Palladium

ome
ainment
omewood Ave

De Longpre Ave

HOLLYWOOD

Sunset Boulevard

Sunset-Gower Studios

Sunset Bronson Studios

N Van Ness Ave

Sunset Boulevard

De Longpre Ave

Helen Bernstein High School

Fernwood Ave

N Serrano Ave

Hobard Blvd

De Longpre Ave

Fountain Avenue

N Ardmore Ave

Normandie Ave

N Mariposa Ave

3

Fountain Avenue

Fountain Avenue

Lexington Avenue

Vine Street

Gordon Street

Tamarind Ave

N Bronson Avenue

La Mirada Ave

Lexington Avenue

Virginia Ave

North Wilton Place

La Mirada Ave

Lexington Avenue

Virginia Ave

Hobard Blvd

N Kingsley Dr

Santa Monica Boulevard

Eleanor Avenue

Romaine Street

oughby Ave

Vine Street

N El Centro Avenue

N Gower Street

Abbey of the Psalms

HOLLYWOOD FOREVER CEMETERY

Cathedral Mausoleum

Paramount Pictures

Camerford Ave

Astroburger

Clark Mausoleum

North Ridgewood Place

Sierra Vista Ave

Romaine St

Barton Ave

Lemon Grove Ave

Monroe St

Marathon St

2

the King
Catholic
Ave

Melrose Avenue

N Arden Blvd

N Luceme Blvd

N Larchmot Blvd

N Gower Street

N Beachwood Dr

N Plymouth Blvd

N Windsor Blvd

N Irving Blvd

N Bronson Ave

Raleigh Studios Hollywood

N Van Ness Ave

North Wilton Place

Clinton Street

Rosewood Ave

Melrose Avenue

Clinton Street

W Maplewood Ave

Rosewood Ave

N Norton Ave

Elmwood Ave

Elmwood Ave

1

BOA Steakhouse **A3**
Cafe Med **B3**
Capitol Records Building **E4**
Chateau Marmont **B3**
Felix in Hollywood **E4**
The Grove **C1**
Hollywood Bowl **C5**
Hollywood Walk of Fame **C/D/E4**
The Laugh Factory **C3**
Los Angeles County Museum of Art **C1**
Meltdown Comics & Collectibles **C3**
Nick Metropolis Collectible Furniture Market **D2**
Pink's Hot Dogs **D2**
Pearl's Liquor Bar **A3**
Stahl House **B3**
TCL Chinese Theatre **C4**
Viper Room **A3**
The Vista Theater **H4**

E   **F**   **G**   **H**

Slowly cruise the length of Sunset Boulevard and take in the sights, sounds, and smells

So much of your Los Angeles visit will involve driving, but that's very much part of the attraction in this city of cars. Getting stuck in traffic on the freeway occasionally is a given, but at least you have your space, AC, and your own music on – and you are experiencing a classic part of the LA experience.

Aside from the iconic **Pacific Coast Highway**, one of the most enjoyable drives in Los Angeles is simply cruising the length of **Sunset Boulevard**. To cover the whole of it will take a couple of hours. Driving from east to west is best, especially if you time it for late afternoon as the sun starts to set and you can envision yourself in your own movie.

The road starts in Silver Lake (see page 143) at Hillhurst Avenue and continues about 22 miles (35km) through **Little Armenia, Hollywood, West Hollywood, Beverly Hills, Westwood, Brentwood, Pacific Palisades,** and finally ends when it meets the PCH. In other words, you are passing through some of Los Angeles' nicest, most attractive areas. You'll pick up a bit of speed towards the end, but for the most part, through a combination of speed limits, traffic, and lights, you'll just be cruising, allowing plenty of time to enjoy the ride.

The best part without a doubt,

though, starts as you go under the 101 freeway. This is the heart of Hollywood, the Sunset Strip, decked out with bright neon lights and flashy signs. This is where gangsters and Old Hollywood came to play and much of LA's 1960's rock scene emerged and today, the whole area is still well-known for its music and nightlife. This is perhaps best represented by **Whisky a Go Go** (www.whiskyagogo.com), the legendary music club that once welcomed the likes of The Doors, Janis Joplin, and Led Zeppelin. Any self-respecting rock fan will be paying a visit to this iconic venue, which is still the setting for frequent gigs.

You'll also drive past **The Laugh Factory** (see page 96) where many big names do stand-up shows, and the **The Viper Room** (see page 89), most famous for being the bar that Johnny Depp used to own and River Phoenix died in front of. And you'll also pass the **Chateau Marmont** (see page 88) on the right, although this one is a little hard to spot as it's tucked away, on a hill just off Sunset Boulevard.

If you want to make a stop – one that's possibly more fun for the non-designated driver – visit **Pearl's Liquor Bar** (8909 Sunset Boulevard; tel: 310-360-6800; www.pearlssunset.com; map A3), which has some of the best views of the Strip from its roof terrace, plus a great cocktail list.

Movie spots

The **Vista Theater** (4473 Sunset Drive) was used as the cinema in *True Romance* (1993) and Sunset was cruised by both John Tavolta and Gene Hackman in *Get Shorty* (1995), where they spot fictional movie star Martin Weir eating breakfast at **Café Med** (8615 West Sunset Boulevard). The comic book store seen in *True Romance* is the **Meltdown Comics & Collectibles** at 7522 Sunset Boulevard; tel: 323-851-7223; http://meltcomics.com.

Visit a piece of pop-culture history at the Capitol Records Tower

The **Capitol Records Building** is one of the few instantly recognisable buildings of the Los Angeles skyline, a 13-story tower that resembles a stack of records and was completed in 1956. Located just north of the Hollywood and Vine intersection, it has been designated a Los Angeles Historic-Cultural Monument.

This is the site of the historic Capitol Studios, where legendary artists such as Frank Sinatra, the Beach Boys, Nat King Cole, Sir Paul McCartney, and many more recorded some of the most beloved music in history. The studios have some unique features, such as echo chambers, designed by guitarist and recording innovator, Les Paul. These echo chambers are subterranean concrete bunkers, located 30ft (9 meters) underground, which can provide a distinct reverb that lasts up to five seconds – the effect is perhaps most famously heard on the Beach Boys' classic, *Good Vibrations*.

The building's 90-ft (27-meter) rooftop spire, which resembles the needle on a phonograph, is topped by a red light that continuously blinks the word 'Hollywood' in Morse code. The spire is made into a Christmas tree during the holidays to officially let the residents of Los Angeles know that the festive season has begun. Each year this is usually switched on by a music star or industry celebrity. The building is still very much in use as a corporate HQ, so tours around the inside seldom happen, but it's certainly worth a walk around.

Capitol Records Building; 1750 Vine Street; map E4

Absorb yourself in the exhibits at the Los Angeles County Museum of Art

The **Los Angeles County Museum of Art** (LACMA) attracts nearly a million visitors every year and holds more than 150,000 works, spanning the history of art from ancient times to the present. Located on Wilshire Boulevard in the Miracle Mile vicinity of Los Angeles, it's the largest art museum in the western United States. Inside are countless art exhibits, plus regular feature film and concert series. The latter frequently change, so it's always worth checking the website to see what's on. Among the museum's permanent collection strengths are its holdings of Asian art, Latin American art – ranging from pre-Columbian masterpieces to works by leading modern and contemporary artists – and Islamic art, of which LACMA hosts one of the most significant collections in the world.

Quite possibly one of the best Instagramable spots in LA is the *Urban Light* permanent exhibition, located outside at LACMA's Wilshire Boulevard entrance. Sculpted by Chris Burden, it first opened in 2008 and consists of 202 restored cast iron street lamps from the 1920s and 1930s. Most of them once lit the streets of Southern California.

Another, very similar, permanent installation outside of LACMA is *Levitated Mass* – a large-scale sculpture by Michael Heizer consisting of a 340-ton (30,8443-kg) boulder affixed above a concrete trench, through which visitors may walk. The nature, expense, and scale of the installation made it an instant topic of discussion within the art world. Like *Urban Light*, the piece is open to the public during museum hours and does not require museum admission.

Los Angeles County Museum of Art; 5905 Wilshire Boulevard, tel: 323-857-6000; www.lacma.org/; map C1

Stand in the footprints of the stars at the TCL Chinese Theatre

Grauman's Chinese Theatre, known under naming rights as TCL Chinese Theatre, is, in essence, an elaborate cinema that sits on the historic Hollywood Walk of Fame. It was originally known as Grauman's Chinese Theatre and renamed Mann's Chinese Theatre in 1973. In 2013, Chinese electronics manufacturer TCL Corporation purchased the facility's naming rights. Regardless of corporate sponsorship, it has been a centrepiece of Hollywood culture since it was built in 1926, serving as the theatre of choice for many movie premieres at the time and even up to the present day. *Star Wars* (1977) first opened here and several Academy Award ceremonies have been held in its auditorium.

But movie buff history aside, the theater's biggest draw is that the concrete in front of the building has preserved the hand and footprints of hundreds of celebrities and movie stars from the very earliest days of the industry. There are nearly 200 Hollywood celebrity handprints, footprints, and autographs in the concrete of the theatre's forecourt.

Some quirky variations of this honoured tradition include C-3PO and R2-D2, imprints of the eyeglasses of Harold Lloyd, the cigar of Groucho Marx, the wands used by Harry Potter stars, and the legs of Betty Grable. Western stars William S. Hart and Roy Rogers left imprints of their guns. Herbie, the Volkswagen Beetle, left the imprints of his tires. The hoofprints of Champion the 'wonder horse', the horse of Gene Autry, and 'Trigger', the horse of Rogers, were left in the concrete beside the prints of the stars who rode them in the movies.

TCL Chinese Theatre; 6925 Hollywood Boulevard; www.tclchinesetheatres.com; map C4

Find your favorite celebrity's star on the Hollywood Walk of Fame

Moving on from looking at movie star handprints, the next pilgrimage point for most people visiting Hollywood is to check out the more than 2,600 five-pointed terrazzo and brass stars that make up the **Hollywood Walk of Fame** (map C/D/E4), which stretches along the sidewalks of 15 blocks of Hollywood Boulevard and three blocks of Vine Street in Hollywood. The stars are permanent public monuments to achievement in the entertainment industry, bearing the names of a mix of actors, musicians, directors, producers, musical and theatrical groups – and even fictional characters – and attracts about 10 million visitors each year.

With so many stars lining the Walk of Fame, you could easily miss the one or two you're really looking for. You can buy a fold-out map at outlets on Hollywood Boulevard with a complete list of every star that has a star. But the easiest way is probably just to look online. The website http://hwof.com/stars provides the address of each notable name, plus a few useful facts and the latest news about that particular celebrity.

Eat at the BOA Steakhouse, a sophisticated Hollywood hot spot

Go big or go home, as the saying goes. This flagship outlet of **BOA Steakhouse** showcases the best of their carnivorous offerings – and it's highly unlikely you'll go home hungry, given the size of the portions. Highlights here include a selection of prime Omaha beef, the 40 day, dry-aged New York strip and the 'Bone In' rib eye, as well as certified organic beef and premium American Wagyu, all served with a choice of rubs and house made sauces. However, the must-sample is in fact the Caesar salad, prepared tableside and consistently the subject of glowing reviews.

This is an upmarket place, with a dress code and attentive service to match. Go for a special meal and you're unlikely to be disappointed. The menu also offers tempting poultry dishes and superb seafood options, a wide variety of sandwiches and salads at lunchtime, an extensive cocktail menu, and an award-winning wine list. Specialty Club Room cocktails include the BOA 405, a tasty libation of vodka, strawberries, balsamic vinegar, lemon, and cracked pepper.

Located in a stylish commercial building at the west end of the Sunset Strip in West Hollywood, this eatery attracts a classy clientele and it wouldn't be all that unusual to see some TMZ photographers hanging about outside to snap an emerging celebrity.

For guests' ease, BOA Steakhouse offers valet parking for $13 with validation.

BOA Steakhouse; 9200 Sunset Boulevard #650; tel: 310-278-2050; www.boasteak. com; map A3

Take a step back in time on Philip Mershon's Felix in Hollywood Tour

Within a quarter-mile radius of Sunset Boulevard and Gower Street, where high-rises have become headstones for long-gone landmarks, local Hollywood historian Philip Mershon invites you to tread the hallowed grounds of Tinseltown's trailblazers on his **Felix in Hollywood** tour. Using minimal props, just some old photos and his own storytelling ability, he conjures up a lively recreation of everything from the first picture studio to the growth of the original Columbia and Warner Bros backlots. His entire tour of Hollywood manages to avoid all references to the Walk of Fame and the Hollywood Sign, but by the end of the tour, you'll have visited nearly all of the places where the major Hollywood studios and productions were born.

Adding a poignant touch, you will see that many of the buildings on the tour are in a state of disrepair, gone, or repurposed. Despite this, the birthplace of Hollywood is brought back to life during this enchanting walking tour. It's certainly a trip down memory lane. Those looking to tick off attractions will probably not find what they're looking for. But for everyone else, it's possibly the most meaningful tour in Hollywood, drawing connections with the early years of Hollywood and the history of the entertainment industry, all in under two hours. Phillip himself has spent over 20 years as a costume supervisor and producer for both movies and TV productions and as he says on the site, 'If my TV only picked up TCM, I'd be happy.'

Tours are open to anyone over the age of 15 and the cost is $40 per ticket. The tour is on foot, so you'll need to park. There is a public parking garage at 1625 Vine Street, a block and a half away from the designated meeting place (1500 Vine Street), where tours depart promptly.

http://felixinhollywoodtours.com; map E4

Feel fancy and take tea at the Chateau Marmont Hotel

It's very easy to miss this iconic Hollywood landmark, especially if you're driving west along Sunset Boulevard (see page 80) because the **Chateau Marmont** is set back from the road, on the right hand side, up a hill and up a small road, Marmont Lane. Set in a 1920s French castle-like building, this iconic, upscale hotel is renowned for its high-profile, celebrity guests. Consequently, if you plan a visit here, don't dress like a tourist. To give an idea of the level we're talking about, a standard room starts at $435 per night, before you get the suites, cottages, bungalows and penthouses. A one-bed penthouse starts at $2,700 per night.

Since it opened in 1927, celebrities as varied as James Dean, Judy Garland, and Lindsay Lohan have stayed at the hotel. But the only celebrity to never check-out was John Belushi, star of the *Blues Brothers* (1980) and *Animal House* (1978), who died in bungalow #3, on March 5th, 1982, after injecting a speedball; a combination of cocaine and heroin. More recently, Sofia Coppola shot the entirety of her movie, *Somewhere* (2010) at the hotel, capturing its reputation as a Hollywood celebrity retreat.

The best way to take this all in is to simply enjoy a nice cup of tea and people-watch for an hour. There is a good chance of spotting a celebrity, or at least absorbing something of the lives of the rich and famous. Just remember not to take photographs, of anything, or anyone, even of yourself, as the staff will come down on you like a ton of bricks.

Chateau Marmont; 8221 Sunset Boulevard; tel: 323-656-1010; www.chateaumarmont. com; map B3

Catch a live band and sip whiskey at the Viper Room

About 10 blocks down from the Chateau Marmont is the site of another famous Hollywood drug overdose, the **Viper Room**, the live music club where River Phoenix died of an overdose in 1993. During the 1990s, the club was known for being a hangout of the Hollywood elite, largely because many of them would stay at the Chateau Marmont Hotel, but the building itself has been a club of sorts since it was built in the 1950s.

It was originally a jazz bar called the Melody Room, a hangout of famous Los Angeles mobsters Bugsy Siegel and Mickey Cohen. After Johnny Depp bought it in 1993 and renamed it the Viper Room, it quickly became popular with young actors and musicians. Regulars included Courtney Love, Jared Leto, Angelina Jolie, Adam Duritz, and Leonardo DiCaprio. Depp himself lived in an apartment just across the road.

These days it's less of a celebrity draw, probably because the intimate venue would be packed full of paparazzi. But up and coming bands still play, so if you're into metal, punk rock, or alternative rock, it's well worth a visit.

Even if you're not there to catch a gig, there is also a worthwhile diversion downstairs: an impressive whiskey bar. The whiskey bar boasts a diverse selection, ranging from the usual tipples to rarer and local whiskeys, including numerous examples of those produced in small batches.

The Viper Room; 8852 Sunset Boulevard; tel: 310-358-1881; http://viperroom.com; map A3

Look out over Los Angeles from the iconic Stahl House

The **Stahl House** is a modernist-styled house designed by architect Pierre Koenig in the Hollywood Hills above Sunset Boulevard. It is also known as Case Study House #22, having been built in 1959 as part of the Case Study Houses program. Today, it is perhaps the most famous representation of a mid-century modern house in the world. The pool, perched on the edge of a cliff, and the futuristic glass box shape of the living room, captured in a renowned Julius Shulman photograph, are examples of the striking modern drama of the house – and even if you don't know the name, you may find on seeing it that you recognise it from somewhere.

The house has been used in numerous fashion shoots, films, advertising campaigns, movies, and TV series, but perhaps most notably in *Galaxy Quest* (1999), as the home of Tim Allen's character. It was listed on the National Register of Historic Places in 2013.

Tours are kept to a small number of guests and vehicles to minimise the impact to the neighbours and increase the enjoyment of guests. Tours start at $60 per person/per car for an afternoon tour, or $35 each for two or more people/per car. Alternatively, it's $90 per person/per car or $50 each for two or more/per car for an evening tour. Photography is allowed with a signed release and only cell phone cameras are permitted. All other cameras or motion cameras (i.e. video, digital, etc.) are not allowed. You can book through the website, which contains details about where to park. Tours usually run twice a week, but even that can vary. It is worth visiting here, though, not only to see a beautiful example of modernist Los Angeles architecture, but also because it's probably one of the most desirable houses in the whole of the Hollywood Hills.

Stahl House, Case House 22; 1635 Woods Drive; https://stahlhouse.com; map B3

Shop for unusual home accessories at the eclectic Nick Metropolis Collectible Furniture Market

If you've ever dreamed of having one or two quirky street signs or even old movie props hanging in your man cave, the garage, or even pride of pace in the dining room, then a visit to **Nick Metropolis Collectible Furniture Market** is a dream come true.

This is truly a sanctuary for salvaged signage and offers everything from traffic lights and metallic construction signs to aluminum letters in every size and color. For more than 20 years, its eponymous owner and appraiser has been collecting and refurbishing midcentury furniture and large-scale signage, such as the light-up replica of the Hollywood Sign, reclaimed from a chain of Hollywood Video stores in Austin and recently purchased by Miley Cyrus.

But this retreat for all things retro isn't just for starlets and movie studios. New knick-knacks and affordable Art Deco oddities are stocked daily, and with a free delivery service,

you just may end up going home with a Hollywood sign for your living room. Unfortunately, as a result of rising rent costs, Nick's market is potentially facing closure. So, do pop by, because there should be more places like this in Los Angeles and if this one disappears, it will be sorely missed. Wander through the positively jam-packed isles crammed full of curiosities. There's stuff laid out indoors and outdoors and it will take quite a while to take everything in. Nowhere else on Earth offers the chance to own a slice of American pop-culture from the halcyon heydays of Hollywood. Parking is on the street, but you should be able to find a spot on La Brea or around the corner on S Sycamore Avenue.

Nick Metropolis Collectible Furniture Market; 100 S. La Brea Avenue, Hancock Park; tel: 323-934-3700; http://nickmetropolis.com; map D2

Make like a Kardashian and shop 'til you drop at The Grove

The Grove is a renowned shopping, dining, and entertainment destination with stores from Brandy Melville to Barneys New York and Swarovski to Sephora. Laid out in the style of a largely pedestrianized outdoor mall, the buildings have been designed in the style of historic LA buildings, set around plazas, courtyards, and groomed topiary. This slick space is often crowded, with residents and tourists alike making their way here for all their fashion and entertainment needs. Celebrity product promotional events are frequently held here and so your chances of spotting – and keeping up with – a Kardashian are reasonably good.

Within the retail section there are a number of restaurants including **Blue Ribbon Sushi Bar & Grill** and **The Cheesecake Factory**, plus a 14-screen cinema. But The Grove forms just part of this large and popular complex, as located directly opposite is a farmer's market – there's even a tram that runs between the two, taking what is actually a totally walkable six minutes.

This is the oldest **farmer's market** in Los Angeles, dating back to the 1930s after the area was first developed as farmland, before becoming oil fields. There are many, many different types of food on offer, from seafood to Spanish, Greek to German, and American to Asian. In addition to the many grocers, there are boutique stores offering beauty and personal products, clothing, flowers, gifts, houseware...more than enough to keep you happily meandering through all the little alley ways for an afternoon. There's valet parking and self-parking, each rising incrementally but with a $24 daily maximum.

The Grove and Original Farmer's Market; 189 The Grove Drive; tel: 323-900-8080; www.thegrovela.com and www.farmersmarketla.com; map C1

Enjoy a live music performance sitting outside on a summer evening at the Hollywood Bowl

The distinctive design of the **Hollywood Bowl** has made it an iconic music venue, instantly recognized around the world. The site was chosen in 1919 since the shaded canyon and popular picnic spot known as 'Daisy Dell' in Bolton Canyon already formed a natural amphitheater. The 'bowl' refers to the shape of the concave hillside the amphitheater is carved into. Anybody who is anybody has played here, from The Doors to Elton John, the Rolling Stones, and Lady Gaga. The distinctive set of concentric arches that form its band shell have been specifically designed to provide an amazing acoustic experience, combined with an extremely sophisticated electronic system, which incorporates micro-second time delay technology to ensure the sound reaches everyone in the venue at the right time.

There are three types of seating at the Bowl: Box Seats – canvas-covered collapsible chairs in groups of four or six surrounded by wooden partitions; SuperSeats – stadium-style plastic seats molded for comfort, with built-in cup holders and set in the center of the audience; and Bench Seats – that start right next to the Terrace boxes and go all the way to the back of the theater. Large video screens on both sides of the stage provide an intimate experience, no matter where you sit. Around the venue itself are a couple of restaurants, but depending on the type of event you're watching, you can quite often bring in your own food and wine.

Parking is limited at the venue. There are four on-site lots and prices range from $18–50. There are however, a number of park and ride options dotted around the area. So this is worth considering to avoid getting stuck in traffic once the event is over. Handily, the LA Metro is rapidly expanding and currently the bowl can be accessed by No. 237/656 Local (from San Fernando Valley or LA basin) and No. 222 Local (from West Hills, Burbank, and Hollywood).

Hollywood Bowl; 2301 Highland Avenue; tel: 323-850-2000; www.hollywoodbowl. com; map C5

Visit Getty's contribution to the LA arts and culture scene at the Getty Center

Not to be confused with the Getty Villa (see page 32) although that is also part of the Getty Museum and consequently the Getty Trust, the **Getty Center** branch of the Museum features pre-20th-century European paintings, drawings, illuminated manuscripts, sculpture, and decorative arts; and 19th- and 20th-century American, Asian, and European photographs. Designed by architect Richard Meier, the $1.3 billion Center sits atop a hill with staggering views all around. It is connected to the visitors' parking garage at the bottom of the hill by a three-car, cable-pulled hovertrain funicular and includes special provisions to address concerns regarding earthquakes and fires.

There are both permanent exhibitions and temporary ones, which often feature major artists, such as the 2017 retrospective of David Hockney's self-portraits. The North Pavilion offers paintings dating up to 1600, as well as a range of medieval and Renaissance sculpture and decorative arts. The East Pavilion features primarily 17th-century baroque art, including a collection of Dutch, French, Flemish, and Spanish paintings, plus sculpture and Italian decorative arts dating from 1600–1800. Head to the South Pavilion for 18th-century paintings and the majority of the Museum's European decorative arts collection, dating up to 1800. And finally, the West Pavilion boasts sculpture and Italian decorative arts of the 1700s through to 1900, as well as 19th-century paintings.

In addition, the fabulous grounds are home to a collection of sculpture as well as the ever-evolving Central Garden: a collection of walkways, planned gardens, and fountains set over 134,000 sq ft (12,449 sq m). With great views out over the city and many shady areas, you could easily spend a day at the Center exploring both the outdoor space and the indoor art.

There's also a very stylish **restaurant** that offers full service in an elegant setting with views of the Santa Monica Mountains. The menu changes seasonally, but a useful gauge for the kind of cuisine is always the wine list. A selection of pinots, cabernets, and zinfandels are available at a wide price range, and everything is from California. Admission is free and parking is $15, or $10 after 3pm.

Getty Center; 1200 Getty Center Drive; tel: 310-440-7300; www.getty.edu/visit/center; map page 100 C1

Tickle your funny bone and catch a big-name comedian doing stand-up at the Laugh Factory

Seinfeld, Richard Pryor, and Robin Williams have all played here since it opened in 1979. The club was founded by Jamie Masada, a major force in the comedy scene who continues to be responsible for launching new comics' careers.

It's a great venue for comedy and can seat up to 600. There's only one stage, which is comprised of two seating sections, banquettes in the back and tables and chairs closer to the stage. There's a second, smaller VIP area with a wrapa-round balcony for premiere show seating. This fully enclosed space boasts a private bar and large wall-mounted plasma screens for private enjoyment of the show.

The club has evolved into a chain, with a number of venues around now around the US and a second Laugh Factory down in Long Beach (see page 152) at 151 S. Pine Avenue, but this venue in Hollywood was the first and is still the most iconic. Since it's located on Sunset Boulevard (see page 80) parking might be a bit tricky, so you'll have to be resourceful. Just be aware of fire hydrants and parking zones with specific times.

Just three blocks up from the Chateau Marmont is the venue that draws the biggest names in comedy. **The Laugh Factory** features many big names like Tim Allen, Kevin Nealon, and even Tom Arnold, among a large regulars list. It's always worth checking the website to see who's playing. In the past, comic greats like Eddie Murphy, Ellen DeGeneres, Jerry

The Laugh Factory; 8001 Sunset Boulevard;
http://laughfactory.com; map C3

Become your own Prince of Bel-Air and explore the single most exclusive suburb in all of North America

'Now this is a story all about how my life got flipped turned upside down...' To a generation, this famous Will Smith opening credits rap is the first thing that comes to mind when **Bel-Air** is mentioned – but this is indeed as posh and exclusive a residential area as you're going to find anywhere. Incidentally, the house that was used for the exterior shots in the *Fresh Prince of Bel-Air* is at 805 St Cloud Road, but you probably won't see much since it's at the end of a gated driveway.

The community was founded in 1923 by Alphonzo Bell, who owned farm property in Santa Fe Springs. When oil was discovered in the area, he invested in a large ranch on what is now Bel-Air Road. He later decided to subdivide the property into large residential lots. Because this area wasn't over-developed and carried certain exclusivity due to the narrow, winding roads, it soon became the location of choice for the mega-wealthy. Today, the likes of Jennifer Aniston and Elon Musk live here, while it was once home to Elizabeth Taylor and Ronald Reagan.

Since you're in the neighborhood, check out the **Hotel Bel-Air**. Set on a 12-acre (4.8ha) site, this 1922 Spanish mission-style luxury boutique hotel features chic, mid-century-inspired rooms with garden entrances. Some rooms also offer fireplaces, infinity pools, patios and/ or balconies, and – naturally – the suites also feature living rooms and Jacuzzis. While actually staying there might be a little on the pricey side, it's worth sticking your head inside and maybe even just indulging in a spot of lunch. If you do, you should definitely dress smartly.

Austrian-born American celebrity chef **Wolfgang Puck** has created the menu at the Hotel Bel-Air and the restaurant bears his name. It features modern California cuisine with European and Mediterranean influences in a spectacular garden setting. The menu changes seasonally, but expect prime cuts and high prices.

Hotel Bel-Air; 701 Stone Canyon Road; tel: 310-472-1211; http://dorchestercollection. com; map page 100 D1

NORTH HOLLYWOOD AND THE SAN FERNANDO VALLEY

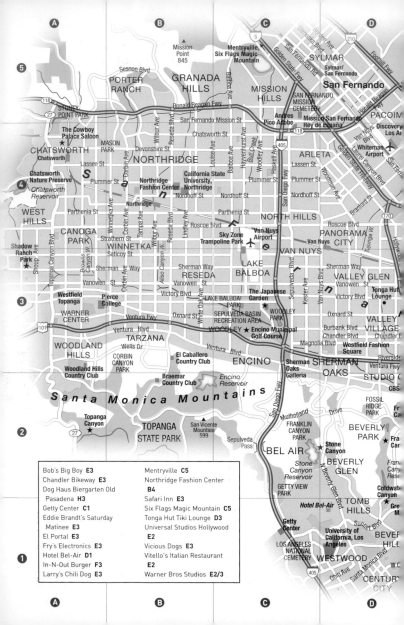

A   B   C   D

5

Mission Point 845

SYLMAR
Sylmar/ San Fernando
San Fernando

PORTER RANCH
GRANADA HILLS
MISSION HILLS
Mentryville, Six Flags Magic Mountain

Sesnon Blvd

Ronald Reagan Fwy

San Fernando Mission St
Chatsworth St

SAN FERNANDO MISSION CEMETERY
Andres Pico Adobe
Mission San Fernando Rey de España

PACOIM
Van Nuys Blvd
Discovery
Los An

The Cowboy Palace Saloon

STONEY POINT PARK

CHATSWORTH
Chatsworth

MASON PARK
Devonshire St

NORTHRIDGE

ARLETA
Whiteman

Chatsworth Nature Preserve
4
Chatsworth Reservoir

Lassen St
Plummer St

California State University, Northridge

Lassen St
Plummer St
Plummer St

WEST HILLS

Parthenia St
Northridge Fashion Center
Northridge

NORTH HILLS

Nordhoff St
Nordhoff St
Nordhoff Ave

Parthenia St
Parthenia St

CANOGA PARK

Roscoe Blvd
Roscoe Blvd

Shadow Ranch Park

WINNETKA
Strathern St
Saticoy St

Sky Zone Trampoline Park
Van Nuys Airport
VAN NUYS
PANORAMA CITY

3
Westfield Topanga
Pierce College

Sherman Way
Vanowen St

LAKE BALBOA

Sherman Way
Vanowen St
VALLEY GLEN
Tonga Hut Lounge

WARNER CENTER

RESEDA
Victory Blvd
LAKE BALBOA PARK

Victory Blvd
VALLEY VILLAGE

Ventura Fwy
Ventura Blvd
Oxnard St

SEPULVEDA BASIN RECREATION AREA
WOODLEY
WOODLEY PARK

Oxnard St
Burbank Blvd
Chandler Blvd
Chandler B

WOODLAND HILLS
TARZANA
Wells Dr

Encino Municipal Golf Course

Magnolia Blvd
Westfield Fashion Square

Woodland Hills Country Club

CORBIN CANYON PARK
El Caballero Country Club

Ventura Blvd
ENCINO

Riverside
Ventura Fwy

Sherman Oaks Galleria
SHERMAN OAKS
STUDIO C
CBS

Braemar Country Club
Encino Reservoir

FOSSIL RIDGE PARK
Fr Ca

Santa Monica Mountains

Mulholland
Drive

FRANKLIN CANYON PARK
BEVERLY PARK
Fra Car

2
Topanga Canyon
San Vicente Mountain 599
Sepulveda Pass

BEL AIR
Stone Canyon

TOPANGA STATE PARK

Stone Canyon Reservoir
BEVERLY GLEN
Fran Cany Rese

GETTY VIEW PARK

Hotel Bel-Air

Coldwater Canyon
Gre

TOMB HILLS

Getty Center

University of California, Los Angeles
BEVEF HILL

LOS ANGELES NATIONAL CEMETERY
WESTWOOD
Sunset Blvd

1

Ohio Ave
Santa Monica Blvd
W.C.
CENTUF

A   B   C   D

Bob's Big Boy **E3**
Chandler Bikeway **E3**
Dog Haus Biergarten Old Pasadena **H3**
Getty Center **C1**
Eddie Brandt's Saturday Matinee **E3**
El Portal **E3**
Fry's Electronics **E3**
Hotel Bel-Air **D1**
In-N-Out Burger **F3**
Larry's Chili Dog **E3**

Mentryville **C5**
Northridge Fashion Center **B4**
Safari Inn **E3**
Six Flags Magic Mountain **C5**
Tonga Hut Tiki Lounge **D3**
Universal Studios Hollywood **E2**
Vicious Dogs **E3**
Vitello's Italian Restaurant **E2**
Warner Bros Studios **E2/3**

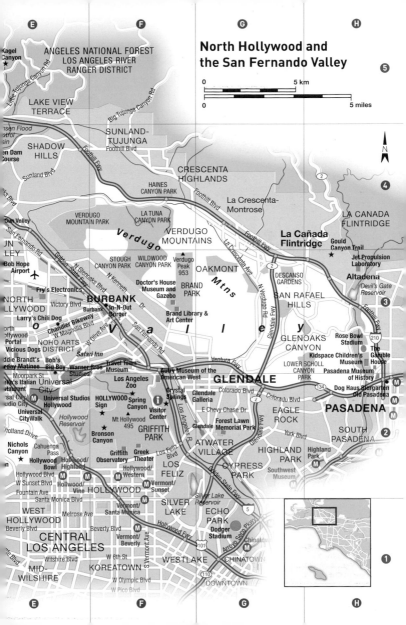

Spend a day exploring the Universal Studios Park

Universal Studios is full-on theme park, much like Warner Brothers (see page 104) and Disneyland (see page 159), so you'll be spending at least a whole day here, possibly even two. It combines a real working studio and behind-the-scenes tours with amusement park attractions. Ticket prices start at $105 for a basic, one-day pass – there are a multitude of options including VIP, Front Line, Two-Day Special Offer, and so on – so you'll want to spend a whole day there to get your money's worth. But you certainly won't struggle to find things to do here.

Currently, the attractions include two Harry Potter rides as part of the relatively new Wizarding World of Harry Potter; the immersive Walking Dead attraction, where you have to outrun zombies; Fast & Furious – Supercharged, where you 'ride along' on a simulated high-speed car chase augmented by incredible 3D graphics; Jurassic Park: The Ride, a great log-flume ride that ends with a sudden drop; Shrek: 4-D, a cinematic fairytale adventure that puts you in the action; WaterWorld, where the movie comes to life in a wave of spectacular stunts and explosions; and the horrifying Revenge of the Mummy ride.

In addition, there's rides drawing on *The Simpsons*, *Transformers*, and *Despicable Me* rides. But don't miss the Studio Tour. On this one you can visit 13 city blocks on four acres (1.6ha) of historic studio lot in the largest set construction project in studio history, built with creative consultation from Steven Spielberg himself. This bad boy includes King Kong 3-D, an intense immersive ride that puts you in the middle of a pack of carnivorous dinosaurs and

the beast himself. You drive past the recreated wrecked Boston suburb where the 747 crashed in the *War of the Worlds* remake (2005); see Wisteria Lane from ABC's hit series *Desperate Housewives* (2004); visit Norman Bates at the legendary Bates Motel from *Psycho* (1960); and of course, come face to face with Jaws.

There's a ton of places to enjoy lunch or dinner, or both. From Krusty Burger to Moe's Tavern (yes, really), to Luigi's Pizza or even Mel's Diner from *American Graffiti* (1973), there is no shortage of themed dining. Parking starts at $20 and there are a number of options available that will cost a little more. Many of the hotels nearby offer deals including park tickets, which is an option if you want to stay a bit closer.

www.universalstudioshollywood.com; map E2

Tap into your film and TV fandom at the Warner Brothers Studios

You might be a little theme-parked-out by now, but the **Warner Brothers Studios** experience is slightly different. There aren't any rides in the traditional sense. Instead, a highlight of this studio odyssey is the Prop Department – home to more than 450,000 registered artifacts, from *Casablanca* (1942) to *The Hangover* (2009), displayed in arguably the largest prop department in the world. You can also see an exhibition of Batmobiles, from the drop-dead gorgeous specimen from *Batman* (1989) to the Tumbler from *Batman Begins* (2005), right up to the most recent Batmobile in its Ben Affleck incarnation.

In addition, you can take a tour of the backlot, which has been the exterior set for many classic films and TV shows, or you can enter some of the soundstages to see where many of the current hit shows are made, including *The Ellen DeGeneres Show*, *The Big Bang Theory*, and *Lethal Weapon*. There's also a DC Universe exhibition where you can see many of the actual costumes used in the recent movies, plus a copy of the extremely rare Superman #1 comic book, which is worth over $3 million. See also set reconstructions from *Batman v Superman: Dawn of Justice* (2016) and *Suicide Squad* (2016).

There's also what's called Stage 48: Script to Screen. This interactive soundstage explores phases of the film and television production process. You'll also see the Central Perk Café from *Friends* (1994) and the Harry Potter & Fantastic Beasts exhibit, where much like the DC Universe exhibition, you wander through recreated sets and get up close so you can see original props and costumes used in the movies.

The Deluxe Tour, which costs $295, includes a guided tour around all the above, plus a complimentary continental breakfast and three-course lunch in the Commissary Fine Dining Room, which is where all the actors go to eat when they get a break during filming. Parking is on site and costs $12.

3400 W Riverside Drive; tel: 877-492-8687; www.wbstudiotour.com; map E2/3

Visit the best electronics store you've ever seen, then have a hot dog

This one is an odd one, but you simply have to do it, especially if you're in the area. **Fry's Electronics** is a chain retailer known for its vast array of computer hardware, accessories and home appliances. But what makes this particular chain stand out in Los Angeles is that every outlet – there's only nine or so in the whole of Southern California – has a particular, slightly off-the-wall theme. And the one in Burbank (2311 N Hollywood Way; map E3) is by far the best. It's themed like a 1950s sci-fi B-movie, if you can imagine that.

This is no small-scale high street outlet, this is, to all intents and purposes, a warehouse super-store...but on the exterior facade is a 'crashed' UFO, still sticking out of the wall of the building. And it's beautifully built, with bits of debris dotted about on the ground. The mad motif continues inside where there's a giant Gort-esque robot, clearly inspired by the epic *The Day The Earth Stood Still* (1951); a full-size USAF Sabre hanging from the ceiling (the primary fighter aircraft used during the 1950s); and a US Army Jeep from the same era on the shop floor, plus a couple of giant alien-style insects and a giant octopus bursting through one of the interior walls. It really has to be seen to be believed. It totally resets the bar for how to make an electronics store more interesting.

An added bonus is that Fry's does stock an awful lot of very useful and often hard-to-find hardware.

Fry's Electronics, 2311 N Hollywood Way, www.frys.com, tel: 818-526-8100

Top dog

While you're in the neighborhood, pop into **Dog Haus Biergarten** at 3 East Green Street in Pasadena. Key ingredients for the perfect hot dog experience include sunshine, fresh air, and cold beer and you'll find all of these at this eatery. This one has by far the best beer garden-style outdoor eating area in Pasadena. Their signature dog is called the Downtown Dog: it features an all-beef skinless sausage, wrapped in smoked bacon and topped with caramelized onions, sautéed bell peppers, mayo, mustard, and ketchup served in a buttered and griddled Hawaiian bread roll.

Create your own your tour of movie locations and sites from modern pop culture

The whole of Los Angeles is basically a movie set. Be amazed at how, through clever filmmaking,

Fast food in Burbank

There is no denying that America, even California with its devotion to the body beautiful, produces the quintessential fast food. Perhaps the most cult outlet is **In-N-Out Burger**, the wildly popular chain with an emphasis on quality products – find them in Burbank at 761 First Street (map F3). Also local to here is the oldest **Bob's Big Boy** in America, replete with the giant, eye-catching Bob-shaped sign, at 4211 Riverside Drive (map E3). The Beatles once dined here in 1965 – a plaque marks the booth in this classic-style diner that is big on memorabilia. But for a bit of TV location scouting, check out **Larry's Chili Dog**, which has appeared in *The Office*. This is great place to stop and grab a well-deserved bite to eat. Almost everything has a chili theme on the menu from this unassuming yellow-colored kitchen. Popular with many from the nearby movie studios, it offers a number of different options; some even have health warnings, like the Crouching Tiger Hidden Dragon and the Mini Stroke, both of which carry a disclaimer that states they are 'not for people with a heart condition or high cholesterol.' Larry's is located at 3122 W Burbank Boulevard (map E3).

different streets can be made to look like a totally different city. The whole of *Se7en* (1995) is basically filmed around a very small area in the middle of Downtown, but we are made to think it's many different streets in a totally different city. The Santa Monica Mountains even doubled for South Korea in the TV series *M*A*S*H*. A great documentary-movie to watch if you can find it is *Los Angeles Plays Itself* (2003), which goes to great detail about LA's history as a movie location.

There's lots of places to go and check out in the San Fernando Valley, even if it's just to have a quick look or even park and take a quick selfie. The best thing to do is tailor it around your favorite movies and do some research beforehand, but we'll offer a few pointers here.

Burbank is full of locations used for shooting; for instance, the house from *ET* (1982) is at 7121 Lonzo Street, Tujunga and the historic Safari Inn from *True Romance* (1994) is at 1911 W Olive Ave, Burbank.

Heading further west, Esther's Hair Salon in Tarzana at 18360 Ventura Boulevard is where Britney Spears publicly shaved her head. The intersection of Hayvenhurst Ave and Plummer Street, North Hills is where the truck jumps off the road into the concrete creek in *Terminator 2: Judgment Day* (1991), closely followed by Arnold Schwarzenegger. In fact a lot of that movie was filmed around this part of Los Angeles, including the Northridge Fashion Mall (9301 Tampa Avenue).

Spend a day at Six Flags Magic Mountain, home of some of the best rollercoaster rides in the world

This is the mother of all theme parks. With 19 rollercoasters, **Six Flags Magic Mountain** holds the world record for most roller coasters in an amusement park and it attracts over 3.1 million visitors every year. There are separately themed areas within the 262-acre theme park located in the Santa Clarita – each zone featuring its own distinct rides, attractions, and food service venues.

There are a number of big, thrilling rides, if adrenaline is your thing. Apocalypse, where you race through a post-apocalyptic wasteland on a high-speed coaster that drops from 95ft (29 meters); Dive Devil, where you plummet 152ft (46 meters) through the air at 60mph (96.5kmh) for the ultimate skydiving experience; the Viper looping frenzy where you bolt down a snake-like course at 70mph (112.5kmh); and the Twisted Colossus, the world's longest, most innovative hybrid coaster.

There are also moderate and mild rides that might be a bit better suited to smaller children and families. As you would expect, there's a multitude of eating options, from Asian restaurants to Mexican food to Italian to ice cream parlors to all-American diners, like Johnny Rockets. A basic, one-day admission will cost $83 per adult, but it's cheaper if you book in advance online. The quietest times to visit are during the week and off-peak – not during the school holidays or public holidays. Parking is on site and starts at $23, but it's cheaper again if you pay online in advance.

Six Flags Magic Mountain; 26101 Magic Mountain Parkway, Valencia; tel: 661-255-4100; www.sixflags.com/magicmountain; map C5

Tour an old oil ghost town

For a glimpse of Los Angeles' oil-drilling history, take a trip to **Mentryville**, an historic location just off the Golden State Freeway in Newhall. In addition to being underappreciated as a glimpse into this chapter of the city's past, it is also a delightful place to hike, being located at the entrance of scenic Pico Canyon.

Mentryville was a 19th-century oil boomtown that grew up around its oil well, known as 'Pico No. 4'. The first oil strike was on September 26, 1876 and it became the first commercially successful oil well in California as well as the longest running on record, finally being capped in 1990. The Pico Canyon oil field proved to be the richest in the state's history to that time and Mentryville became a boomtown from 1876 to 1900. The town was gradually abandoned and by the 1960s, it was a ghost town.

As you traverse the canyon road, you will come across various oil-drilling paraphenalia, including antique drilling rigs, while you can also visit the preserved buildings that made up Mentryville every other weekend. With its undisturbed frontier feel, it's no surprise that the town has been used as a filming location. Scenes

from *The Color Purple* (1985) were filmed around here along with episodes of *The X-Files*, *The A-Team,* and *Murder, She Wrote*. It is extraordinary to absorb its Old West ambiance, knowing that you are only a couple of miles from bustling Santa Clarita.

As a bonus, the hiking trails that run through here are pretty easy-going and family-friendly – primarily flat, shaded, and ideal for biking. Thoughtful conservation work has added some upgrades such as benches and picnic tables, while parking is plentiful and cheap, at $5.

27201 Pico Canyon Road, Newhall; tel: 661-251-8820, www.scvhistory.com/ mentryville; map C5

Put a different pedal to the metal on the Chandler Bikeway

The **Chandler Bikeway** (map E3) is a hidden gem tucked nicely into a Burbank neighborhood, beginning as a well-maintained corridor that runs in the median between lanes of traffic on Chandler Boulevard. Like the popular Orange Line Bike Path to the west, the trail sits on top of the Southern Pacific's old Burbank Branch railway line. The route through Burbank is surprisingly beautiful, with a wide array of trees, shrubs, and flowerbeds dotting the grounds surrounding the trail.

The first two miles are defined by the quaint and tidy neighborhood that it passes through. The area is made up of unique homes, some with very bright and vibrant paint jobs that remind you that you're in sunny Southern California. The abundance of orange and lemon trees in residents' yards also make for a wonderful sight in the winter. The odd sculpture or piece of street art perks up the surroundings, but the real draw is the path's view of the Verdugo Mountains.

Upon crossing Clybourn Avenue, you have left the city limits of Burbank and entered the Los Angeles neighborhood of North Hollywood – often referred to by the pseudo-modernistic moniker NoHo. The trail now shifts out of the median to the south side of the road, as the surrounding cityscape changes as well from residential neighborhoods to light industrial and retail development.

To reach the eastern trailhead from Interstate 5, take the West Burbank Boulevard exit and take a left onto West Burbank Boulevard. After just 0.3 mile (0.5km), take a left onto Victory Boulevard. Another short quarter-mile and you take a right onto West Chandler Boulevard. The trailhead is again a quarter-mile up Chandler Boulevard, with on-street parking.

To reach the western trailhead from I-5, take the West Burbank Boulevard exit and take a left onto West Burbank Boulevard. After 3.2 miles (5km), take a left onto Vineland Avenue. The trailhead is just a quarter-mile away on the left at the intersection with Chandler Boulevard. Parking is on-street.

Soak up some culture and discover the North Hollywood arts scene

As you head over the hills into the San Fernando Valley, North Hollywood is one of the first districts you'll come to. Its history is linked with the entertainment industry, as thanks to the greater space available, many studios set up shop in the area, but today, NoHo is reaping the atmospheric benefits of the artists and other creatives who have made the **North Hollywood Arts District** a destination for all things cultural. Frequented by a sweet spot blend of bohemians and yuppies, the area is an intriguing place to discover eclectic stores, cafés, and nightlife. Meanwhile, with nearly two dozen intimate theaters and various dance studios, this is a real performing arts hub, while fine artists show their work at local cultural centers. Hang around and you'll see musicians, actors, and more hanging out and working on their craft.

There are many quirky shops to discover in the area, but for film buffs, a visit to **Eddie Brandt's**

Saturday Matinee 5006 Vineland Avenue; tel: 818-506-4242; http://ebsmvideo.com; map E3) is a must. Here you will discover a collection of hard-to-find or even out-of-print movies, although many of them are on VHS. The store opened in 1969 and if you are hopeful of running into other true movie fans, this is the sort of place it might happen. The clerks are happy to be helpful and seek out whatever you've been looking for.

The **El Portal** Art Deco-style theatre (11206 Weddington Street; tel: 818-508-0281; http://elportaltheatre.com; map E3), which opened in 1926 as a silent and vaudeville theater, is another must-see, as is **NoHo Arts District Farmers Market**, selling organic goodies.

A major bonus is that the advent of the Metro Los Angeles has made the district more accessible than ever. You can hop on the red line, head all the way north, and you'll be in the heart of the action.

Treat your taste buds to proper Italian pizza followed by a night of live jazz

Long-standing restaurant **Vitello's** was established in Tujunga Village by Sal Vitello, a baker from New York, and it became a popular hangout for the likes of the Rat Pack. Although it's changed hands a few times since then, Vitello's remains a popular eatery with industry types, who frequently drop in for a plate of pasta and a drink – it's close to CBS Studios Lot and Universal City.

But there are a number of reasons to pay a visit. If you appreciate proper Italian food – and we do mean proper – not this deep-dish-cheese-with-everything nonsense, but pizza cooked the same way as by the people who invented it, then this is a must. Meanwhile, upstairs is very popular jazz club

called the **E-Spot**, which features live performances nightly in an intimate, 120-seat venue. From stand-up comedy to jazz, Latin to R&B, this recently renovated venue regularly attracts big names. A very respectable wine list accompanies an equally respectable menu, with a fairly equal mix of both American and Italian food and wine.

Alternatively, you could retire post-meal to the **Rendition Room**, a speakeasy-style cocktail bar also on the premises, with 1920s decor. Reservations are required and the house rules include the following: no phone calls; no standing at the bar; no talking about politics or religion; and don't even think of ordering a 'Cosmo.' Unless you're a member, each reservation is for a maximum of two hours to help maintain some exclusivity. (Membership is $800 per year and includes a host of benefits, including dinner discounts and access to special functions.) A ticket to the jazz club also guarantees you a table for dinner beforehand, but obviously the cost of dinner is separate.

Vitello's Italian Restaurant; 4349 Tujunga Avenue; tel: 818-769-0905; http://vitellos restaurant.com; map E2

Go full tiki at the Tonga Hut

This delightful tiki bar was opened the height of the mid-century Polynesian culture craze, in 1958, by brothers Ace and Ed Libby – and part of its unique charm today is the way in which this period style has been retained today. After a period of being run down, the **Tonga Hut** was thankfully restored to its former glory. The original water features are once again flowing, the décor is laid out in period-appropriate style, and the jukebox plays a range of vintage tunes. All this is ensuring its continued status as the oldest operating tiki bar in Los Angeles, which shows no signs of slowing down.

Repeat visitors can aim to join the The Loyal Order of the Drooling Bastard, the criteria for which is to order every drink in the Grog Log – which runs to over 80 drinks – within one year. But assuming this isn't possible, you can still enjoy drinks ranging from cheap local beer to classic cocktails made to original recipes. It has more complicated drinks with kooky names than you ever thought existed, but if you somehow thumb through the menu and aren't satisfied, some of the bartenders are willing to mix you up their own original creations. They also occasionally bring in award-winning guest bartenders. It all adds up to one of North Hollywood's most satisfying watering holes.

Tonga Hut; 12808 Victory Boulevard; tel: 818-769-0708 http://tongahut.com; map D3

BEVERLY HILLS

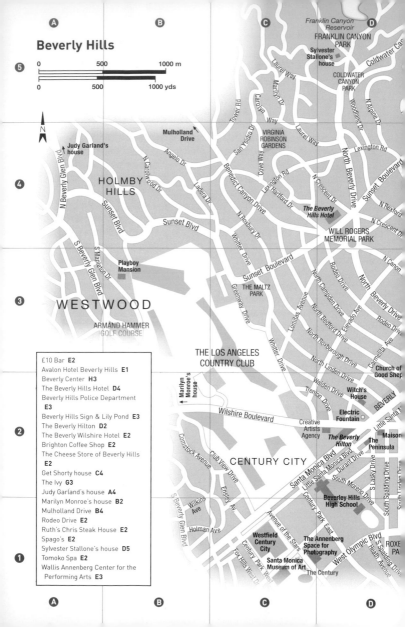

Beverly Hills

0 — 500 — 1000 m
0 — 500 — 1000 yds

FRANKLIN CANYON PARK
Franklin Canyon Reservoir
Sylvester Stallone's house
COLDWATER CANYON PARK
Coldwater Canyon
Laurel Way
Marilyn Dr
Carolyn Way
Virginia Robinson Gardens
Woodland Dr
N Alpine Dr
Lexington Rd
North Beverly Drive
Sunset Boulevard
Mulholland Drive
Angelo Dr
N Carolwood Dr
Ladera Dr
San Ysidro Dr
Cove Way
Lexington Rd
Hartford Dr
N Crescent Dr
The Beverly Hills Hotel
N Rexford
N Crescent Dr
WILL ROGERS MEMORIAL PARK
Judy Garland's house
HOLMBY HILLS
Sunset Blvd
S Beverly Glen Blvd
S Mapleton Dr
Sunset Blvd
Benedict Canyon Drive
N Roxbury Dr
Whitter Drive
Sunset Boulevard
N Canon
Rodeo Drive
North Beverly Drive
Playboy Mansion
THE MALTZ PARK
Lomitas Avenue
North Camden Drive
North Bedford Drive
Elevado Ave
Rodeo Drive
WESTWOOD
Greenway Drive
North Roxborough Drive
Carmelita Ave
ARMAND HAMMER GOLF COURSE
Whitter Drive
North Linden Drive
Church of Good Shep
THE LOS ANGELES COUNTRY CLUB
Walden Drive
Trenton Drive
Witch's House
Electric Fountain
BEVERLY
Little Santa
Marilyn Monroe's house
Wilshire Boulevard
Creative Artists Agency
The Beverly Hilton
Maison
The Peninsula
Comstock Avenue
Club View Drive
Ensley Av
Wilkins Ave
S Beverly Glen Blvd
CENTURY CITY
Santa Monica Blvd
Little Santa Monica Blvd
Durant Drive
South Moreno Drive
S Lasky Drive
South Spalding Drive
Holman Ave
Beverley Hills High School
Avenue of the Stars
Century Park East
Century Park West
Fox Hills West Dr
Westfield Century City
Santa Monica Museum of Art
The Annenberg Space for Photography
West Olympic Blvd
ROXE PA
S Spalding Drive
Heath Avenue
The Century

£10 Bar **E2**
Avalon Hotel Beverly Hills **E1**
Beverly Center **H3**
The Beverly Hills Hotel **D4**
Beverly Hills Police Department **E3**
Beverly Hills Sign & Lily Pond **E3**
The Beverly Hilton **D2**
The Beverly Wilshire Hotel **E2**
Brighton Coffee Shop **E2**
The Cheese Store of Beverly Hills **E2**
Get Shorty house **C4**
The Ivy **G3**
Judy Garland's house **A4**
Marilyn Monroe's house **B2**
Mulholland Drive **B4**
Rodeo Drive **E2**
Ruth's Chris Steak House **E2**
Spago's **E2**
Sylvester Stallone's house **D5**
Tomoko Spa **E2**
Wallis Annenberg Center for the Performing Arts **E3**

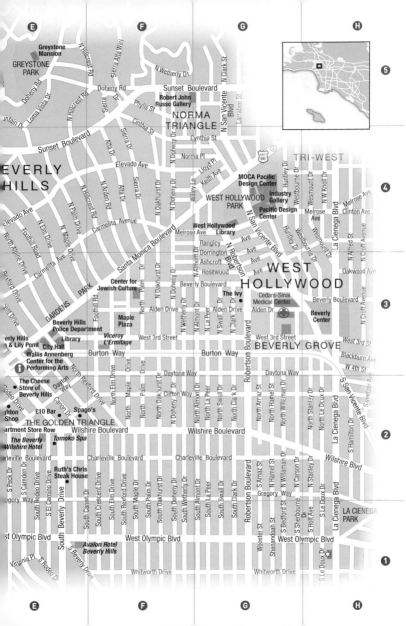

Have your *Pretty Woman* moment on Rodeo Drive

Along with Bond Street and Fifth Avenue, **Rodeo Drive** (map E2) is known the world over for its high profile designer-label stores. Prada, Cartier, Chanel, Gucci, Burberry, and the Louis Vuitton flagship are just a few of the high fashion houses in this super-expensive, pedestrianized shopping district.

It's actually a two-mile-long street located in Beverly Hills, divided as it crosses Santa Monica Boulevard. The longer, north-west side is residential and the shops, restaurants and cafés are on the shorter, south-west side.

It's unlikely you'll see an A-list celebrity out shopping, as most of them have teams of people that do that task for them, but the area also has banks and other businesses essential to daily life, albeit the daily life of very wealthy people. The 'Golden Triangle,' which extends to Wilshire Boulevard, is both a shopping district and a tourist attraction.

Check out http://rodeodrive-bh.com for more information.

The reason everyone knows Rodeo Drive is because this is the location of Julia Roberts' shopping spree and revenge over a snooty sales assistant in *Pretty Woman* (1990): 'Big mistake. Big. Huge!' While many may dream of a shopping spree with someone else's credit card, few are likely to be able to indulge in the high-end boutiques, so window-shopping is the order of the day. Along the $200-million faux cobbled walkway of Two Rodeo, browsing tourists mingle with serious spenders. A hop away is **Anderson Court**, which is the only shopping mall designed by famed American architect, Frank Lloyd Wright.

Movie mania

Rodeo Drive and the nearby area has featured in a number of popular movies, most notably *Pretty Woman* (1990), but also *Down and Out in Beverly Hills* (1986) and *Beverly Hills Cop* (1984), where Eddie Murphy's character is staying at the Beverly Wilshire Hotel (9500 Wilshire Boulevard). The Beverly Hills Police Department building at 464 N Rexford Dr was used in *The Last Boy Scout* (1991) and The Beverly Hilton at 9876 Wilshire Boulevard was used in *Argo* (2012) for the script reading.

Enjoy lunch at celebrity favorite, The Ivy

The Ivy on 113 N Robertson Boulevard – a super-trendy area that nestles between Melrose, Beverly Grove, and Beverly Hills – has long been very popular with local celebrities, such as Sir Patrick Stewart, who cites this as one of his favorites. An article on MSNBC once called The Ivy 'a celebrity beehive that sees a constant stream of Hummers, Mercedes, and Jaguars pull up and discharge folks who pay through the nose to be seen eating in public.' But this does the restaurant a diservice; with its shady, picket-fenced patio, romantic ambiance, and delightful food, The Ivy is also a special place for mere mortals.

While it's not actually as ridiculously expensive as other high-profile restaurants in the area, it can be a little tricky to get a table, especially for dinner. Try going for brunch instead and you should be able to get a table on the spot, provided you go just before or just after the lunchtime rush.

The decor is bright and colorful and the plates, table dressings, and even the seat cushions carry a warm floral motif. Potted flowers are also dotted about and the menu – while traditionally American with dishes like Filet Mignon, Wagyu, lobster, ribs, and lamb – also carries a hint of Italian influence.

There's valet parking or metered parking across the street, or you could park at the **Beverly Center**, a high-end shopping mall one block away.

The Ivy; 113 N Robertson Boulevard; tel: 310-274-8303; www.theivyrestaurants. com; map G3
The Beverly Center; 8500 Beverly Boulevard; tel: 310-854-0070; http://beverlycenter.com; map H3

Buy a map showing the homes of the stars and drive around yourself

For about $10, from any one of a number of vendors on Sunset Boulevard, you can buy a *Map & Guide to Movie Stars Homes & Hangouts*. It mostly covers West Hollywood, Brentwood, Beverly Hills, and Bel Air and it offers a comprehensive drive around the area looking for say, where Judy Garland used to live (924 Bel Air Road, Bel Air; map A4) or Sylvester Stallone (1121 Beverly Drive, Beverly Hills; map D5) or Marilyn Monroe (12305 Fifth Helena Drive, Brentwood; map B2).

Traffic around these high-profile areas is not bad at all. If anything, you'll find yourself cruising along at very moderate speeds, adhering to the speed limit of what is, in essence, a built up, residential neighborhood. Make sure the car is full of gas, pack a couple of bottles of water in the car and off you go. **Santa Monica Boulevard**, however, will be jam-packed during daytime hours, as will **Wilshire Boulevard** to some extent and **Sunset Boulevard**, if not quite so much, so be warned should you decide to jump back on any one of those during your tour.

You'll probably see a few people doing exactly the same thing as you and one of the organized tour buses will probably pass you at least once or twice. If you'd rather hop on one of these, see www.star linetours.com or https://lacitytours.com. The roads are pretty wide and you'll be able to pull up outside each house with little problem.

You will also notice how much construction work there is in the area. This is an ongoing cycle as buyers of many of these beautiful properties prefer to knock down whatever was there when they bought it and then build their own. (Or at the very least, add another two or three bathrooms.) When you think about how many houses there are and how many times they exchange hands, you can understand why you'll see so much building work.

Houses of note include 1011 N Beverly Drive, which was used in *The Bodyguard* (1992), *The Godfather* (1972), and *Fletch* (1985). You won't be able to enter the grounds, as it's closed off by a no-nonsense electric gate, but you'll recognise the style of the structure that is visible. This one is on a particular nasty corner, so be careful when you're pulling in and out. Also, 1017 N Crescent Drive is the house that doubles as Martin Weir's house in *Get Shorty* (1995) although as you'll see, the hedges have grown somewhat, so you can't see in anywhere near as much as at one time.

Catch up with celebrity gossip on a TMZ tour

Instead of finding your own way through the maze of mega-mansions in Beverly Hills, you can take any one of several tours that operate from around Hollywood or Sunset Boulevard. **TMZ** is probably one of the most well-known and tours depart daily from either the **Hard Rock Cafe** (6801 Hollywood Boulevard) or **The Grove** (189 The Grove Drive; see page 92). Adult tickets (age 13 and above) cost $51.50 (£40) and children (ages 2 -12) $41.50 (£32). The ticket desk is located inside the Hard Rock Cafe or in front of the Nike Store at The Grove outdoor shopping mall.

If you like celebrity gossip, then you've probably already heard of TMZ. The name stands for the 30-mile zone, the historic 'studio zone' within a 30-mile (50 km) radius centered at the intersection of West Beverly Boulevard and North La Cienega Boulevard. Ever since its humble beginnings in 2005, it has quickly grown to be one of the most popular sources of salacious celebrity gossip and film-star scandal, attracting the world's attention when it was the first to break the story that actor Mel Gibson had been arrested for driving under the influence.

There's no difference between the two tours, aside from the start and end point. Each one is approximately two hours long, but may run slightly shorter or longer due to traffic or other unforeseen circumstances. Each tour has a TMZ Guide sharing inside information about your favorite celebrities and the places they like to go. Along the route, the guide will tell stories and interact with passengers while using video created by TMZ to help give you the history of each location. They will explain how TMZ broke some of the biggest stories in celebrity news, and what it's like to be at the forefront of the celebrity news biz.

TMZ Tour; tel: 844-869-8687; www.tmz.com

Dress up and dine out at Ruth's Chris Steak House

There's an almost infinite number of eateries to choose from in the area surrounding Beverly Hills; from **The Ivy** (see page 119) to **Spago's** (176 N Canon Drive; map E2), Wolfgang Puck's sleek, popular-but-pricey bistro that has been overwhelmingly popular for decades. But don't miss out on **Ruth's Chris Steak House**, which is possibly not what you might expect. It is a collection of local steak houses with over 150 locations worldwide, a fine dining establishment offering USDA Prime steaks with delicious sides and homemade desserts. Do note that the dress code is 'business-casual,' with no t-shirts or sweatshirts allowed. More importantly, it offers one of the best steaks you'll get in Los Angeles.

Back in 1965, a single mother by the name of Ruth Fertel bought a troubled restaurant in New Orleans and trained herself in every part of the business. She hired only single moms as staff and it soon became an underground success, attracting local celebrities. A clause in the original sales agreement prevented her from using the restaurant's name at any other location, so when a fire in her original site caused her to move, she simply changed the name to Ruth's Chris Steak House.

Their trademark is prime steaks seared at 982°C (1,800F) and served on ceramic plates heated to 260°C (500F). Simply seasoned with salt, pepper, and parsley, just before the plates leave the kitchen, a bit of butter is added to create the signature 'sizzle'. Fertel firmly believed that her success was due as much to the sound and smell of the 'sizzle' as well as the taste. 'You hear that sizzle, and you think, 'I wonder if that's my steak,'' she said in an interview shortly before her death.

The mouth-watering menu includes Porterhouse, petite fillet, New York Strip, Cowboy ribeye, and lamb chops as well as Chilean sea bass, lobster, and sautéed New Orleans style shrimp, together with a very respectable, award-winning wine list.

Ruth's Chris Steak House; 224 South Beverly Drive; tel: 310-859-8744; www.ruthschris.com; map E2

Spend a bit more than £10 at the £10 (Ten Pound) Bar

Tucked away on the second floor of the **Montage Beverly Hills** hotel, this speakeasy-themed haunt offers craft cocktails, fine wine, and a secluded outdoor terrace that overlooks **Beverly Canon Gardens**. As the only official US stockist of Macallan single malt Scotch whiskey, it has an impressive selection, each one served in beautiful Lalique crystal glassware, as it should be. Browse the list of Sherry Oak, fine oak, Highland Park and 'old & rare' bottles aged from 15 to up to 64 years. Should you wish to have your drink on the rocks, you've got a choice of ice that's like nothing you've likely seen before: choose from kold-draft cubes, soapstone rocks, a water ball made from water from the Highland Springs, and, finally, the ice sphere with the house £10 logo, all presented on the house cart.

This fancy Scotch bar has an upscale dinner menu, cigars, a patio, a fireplace, and some of the oldest and finest Scotches available for you to sample, along with an endless amount of Hook's 3-year-aged cheddar and pressed strips of bacon. This luxury comes at a price though, there's a $50 per person minimum bar tab, but with $68 Rob Roys and a $40 dram of 15-year-old Macallan Fine Oak, it won't take long to pass that.

Come for the whisky and stay for the food that's on offer, from the Fennel Risotto Balls to the 9oz Dry-Aged New York Striploin. If you just want something small, though, you could always go with the caviar. With a top-notch selection and service, you can also expect some of the best cocktails around. Try the Jimmy Mac, made with Macallan 18-year, Benedictine, Averna, and bitters.

Expect to dish out $30–55 for cocktails and up to $6,400 for a single malt pour. You will need to call ahead to make a reservation as this intimate bar has limited space.

£10 (Ten Pound) Bar; 225 N Canon Drive; tel: 310-906-7218; www.montagehotels. com/beverlyhills/dining/ten-pound; map E2

This tourist thing can take its toll, so relax at the Tomoko Spa

Whether you're treating yourself to a mani/pedi, a soothing massage, or a rejuvenating body therapy, Beverly Hills has world-class spas that offer the very best in pampering services. One such outlet is the **Tomoko Spa**, which takes a healing approach to massage. You'll notice the architecture by Thea Home, which will calm your senses with its minimalist Japanese aesthetic and from the moment you slide into the spa's slippers, you'll already start to feel relaxed.

Tomoko Spa is a five-star experience from beginning to end. After being greeted and led into a waiting room, you're given water, tea, and a tray of irresistible snacks, such as coconut jelly and chocolate truffles. Then, once you enter your private room, complete with its own shower or bath and change into a kimono, a massage therapist provides a foot massage as preparation for the treatment. Privacy is key, here the treatment rooms feature all the amenities you could think of, meaning you don't have to leave to go to a locker room to change. The suites feature massage beds, wooden bath, shower, plus highbrow organic products such as eco-friendly deodorant, face wipes, Oribe hair spray, and more. Each treatment starts with a 15 minute foot soak and rub, to help

relax you and, through reflexology, open up your back muscles. One of the most popular and intriguing treatments is the Zenshin massage (60min, $260), which promotes holistic balance by combining Swedish and Japanese techniques. Small, hot stones are used throughout the treatment as well as warm Japanese sake, which is poured on your back to alleviate muscle tension.

Whatever your needs, the treatments can be customized to suit, and they may just be the best in the city. Every detail is minded and all aches and pains attended to. Owner Tomoko Kurono spent nine years researching and traveling to develop her signature massage and although it's pricey (the Tomoko Massage alone is over $200), it is definitely worth every cent.

Tomoko Spa; 141 S Beverly Drive; tel: 310-205-7300; http://tomokospa.com; map E2

125

Treat your taste buds at the Cheese Store of Beverly Hills

Beverly Hills is a veritable Aladdin's cave of hidden attractions, albeit mostly quite expensive ones, but worth a look nonetheless for the treats they harbor. The **Cheese Store of Beverly Hills** is one such place: a gourmet store renowned for its selection of 500 to 600 cheeses. You can also pick up some wine to go with your cheese, plus other foodie delicacies – even caviar. The store stocks the rarest of all, Golden Imperial Osetra. It also claims to carry 'the largest assortment of goats' and sheep's milk cheeses found anywhere.' Needless to say, the store's owner, Austrian cheese expert Norbert Wabnig, is something of a noted Los Angeles personality.

The store, housed in a refurbished 1920s brick building, has supplied many of Los Angeles' high-end restaurants past and present, including Wolfgang Puck's Spago, Valentino's, Patina, and Bar Marmont, as well as the Bellagio Hotel in Las Vegas. To a Cheese Store newbie, the selection can be overwhelming, but the friendly and knowledgeable staff are always happy to help.

In addition to simply walking in, there are organised tastings one evening every month. These are very popular and sell out quickly; for $65 (£50) per person you can enjoy learning about and tasting all sort of different imported and domestic cheeses, the best wines to pair them with and a whole host of other culinary tidbits of useful info. The store also has a shrewd selection of wines that pair with cheese and enough gourmet goodies to drive any hapless shopper to distraction – caviar, truffles, charcuterie, balsamic vinegar, hazelnut oil, and more. A 48 hour cancellation notice is required and free valet parking is provided.

The Cheese Store of Beverly Hills; 419 N Beverly Drive; tel: 310-278-2855; http://cheesestorebh.com; map E2

Forget the lifestyles of the rich and famous and dive into the history of Beverly Hills

Having spent all your money spoiling yourself on Rodeo Drive, at the £10 bar, or at the Tomoko Spa, what you need is something interesting and more importantly, free, to do next. Beverly Hills is not a city within Los Angeles that you'd normally associate with interesting history, but you'd be surprised. After all, it had to start somewhere.

Before it was known as Beverly Hills, this city offered a wealth of natural resources including oil and water, both precious commodities in Southern California at the time. The city came to be known as Beverly Hills in 1914, a turning point as development of the now-iconic **Beverly Hills Hotel** (www.dorchestercollection.com; map D4) and other buildings brought a new crowd to the area. Movie industry types began to make this their home and Beverly Hills developed a reputation for glamour and luxury that still holds true today. The Love Beverly Hills website offers a self-guided tour that can be downloaded and printed out.

The tour takes you to several iconic historical spots in Beverly Hills to learn about the city's diverse heritage including: the **Wallis Annenberg Center for the Performing Arts** (www.thewallis.org;

map E3), formerly the city's Post Office and built in the classic Italian Renaissance style; the **Beverly Hills Sign & Lily Pond** (map E3), one of the city's first landmarks; and the **Avalon Hotel Beverly Hills** (www.avalon-hotel.com; map E1), formerly the Beverly Carlton Hotel, which was once the residence of Marilyn Monroe. It's also worth having a look at **the Beverly Hilton** (www.beverlyhilton.com; map D2), an iconic hotel and a classic example of mid-century modern architecture and the **Brighton Coffee Shop** (www.brightoncoffeeshop.com; map E2), the oldest coffee shop in Beverly Hills, which opened in the early 1930s.

http://lovebeverlyhills.com

Drive the length of Mulholland Drive

Often mentioned in movies set in Los Angeles and the title of David Lynch's 2001 mysterious master-piece, **Mulholland Drive** (map B4) is the road of classic make out points, Hollywood chase scenes, and scenic splendour. Extending from the Pacific Coast Highway all the way to downtown Holly-wood, this minor two-lane road loosely follows the ridge-line of the Santa Monica Mountains and Hollywood Hills that separate LA from the San Fernando Valley. But while the road itself is not a main thoroughfare, Mulholland Drive is famous not only for its views, but also its mystique.

You can drive it in its entirety while stopping at the half dozen or so overlooks all in less than an hour. This is the big one; 55 miles (88km) long, with eight overlook points, it's the most well-known of Los Angeles' scenic drives. Named for engineer William Mulholland, Mulholland Drive was built in the 1920s to bring housing develop-ments to the Hollywood Hills, and indeed some of the most exclusive homes have appeared along it since then.

You can go in either direction, but it might be fun to drive west into the setting sun after having spent a few hours driving around Beverly Hills, finding the homes of the movie stars (see page 120). Any major canyon road will meet up with Mulholland at some point, but for the best views start from the beginning – where Mulholland meets Cahuenga. If coming from the Valley, travel south on Cahuen-ga Boulevard W and make a right and quick left to climb up Mulhol-land. If coming from Hollywood, take Cahuenga Boulevard E, make

a right on Lakeridge Pl and then a right across the bridge.

It's no wonder the scenic parkway was once a racing hotspot; its sloping curves are as exhilarating as they are perilous. Drive safely, especially through the many blind corners. Two miles down the road, you'll come across the **Universal City Overlook** with its top-down view of Universal Studios and, off in the distance, Warner Bros. Studios. If you have the time, stay on Mulholland past the 405 and bear left at Encino Hills Drive, at which point the road will turn into a cracked, gravelly mess. Wind up the dirt road and eventually you'll reach the entrance to **San Vicente Mountain Park**, set in the Santa Monica Mountains. Climb to the top of the **Cold War radar tower** here for one of the best 360-degree views in the entire county. On clear days, you can see Palos Verdes, Downtown, and the entire valley.

LOS FELIZ AND SILVER LAKE

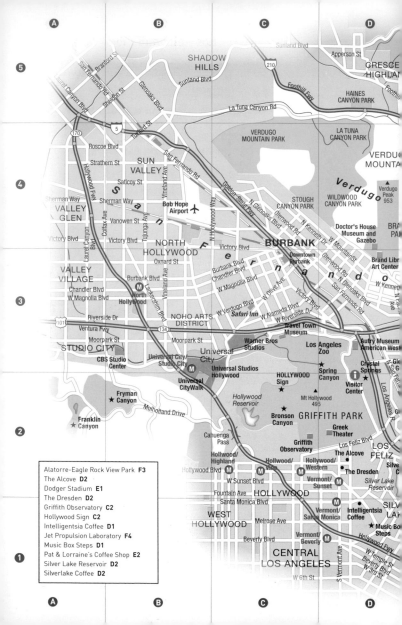

Alatorre-Eagle Rock View Park **F3**
The Alcove **D2**
Dodger Stadium **E1**
The Dresden **D2**
Griffith Observatory **C2**
Hollywood Sign **C2**
Intelligentsia Coffee **D1**
Jet Propulsion Laboratory **F4**
Music Box Steps **D1**
Pat & Lorraine's Coffee Shop **E2**
Silver Lake Reservoir **D2**
Silverlake Coffee **D2**

Walk up the historic Music Box Steps, as seen in the Laurel and Hardy movie

Sometimes the simplest of ideas are the best and the plot of the 1932 short comedy *The Music Box* is very simple indeed. Deliverymen Stan Laurel and Oliver Hardy struggle to push a large crated piano up a seemingly insurmountable flight of stairs. That's it. But it soon turns into a disaster of epic and immensely entertaining proportions. This 29-minute masterpiece won the Oscar for Best Short Subject in 1932, the only such honour bestowed on a Laurel and Hardy film, and also the first short to be so-honoured.

What's almost as funny is how much the number of actual steps varies according to different accounts. The *LA Times* says it's

133, IMDb reckons it's 131 and Wikipedia says it's 147. So be sure to keep an accurate count when you climb them! Located between 923 and 935 Vendome Street, in the Silver Lake district of Los Angeles, it's amazing to imagine the area before it was built up way back in 1932. The mansion at the top of the stairs was not really at the top of the stairs, but was a set on the Hal Roach Studios lot. The actual stairs lead to a cul-de-sac.

When the film was shot, a special police squad had to be on duty at the **Vendome Street staircase** (map D1) for the length of the four-day location shoot to keep more than 3,500 onlookers and fans from interfering with the production. But knowing how to keep the fans happy, Laurel and Hardy reportedly signed about 2,000 autographs in their breaks.

Marked by a plaque on a wall at the bottom, the steps are pretty easy to get to by car. It shouldn't take more than an hour to snap some selfies, appreciate the cinematic history of this location and carefully count how steps there are. But if you're already in the Silver Lake area, it really would be a shame not to stop and pay a little visit.

Have brunch with the stars at the Alcove

A number of celebrities live in the **Loz Feliz** area, so it's not uncommon to catch one or two stars out having brunch on a Sunday afternoon. Not only are there lots of pricey apartments in Loz Feliz, but the maze of private access roads just north of Los Feliz Boulevard is home to a large number of celebrities, from Mel Gibson to Megan Fox and Chris Pine to Christina Ricci. In fact, Los Feliz probably offers the single highest concentration of celebrities in any one area, and it's not at all surprising as this is a super trendy and scenic area.

Housed in two historic bungalows, the **Alcove** is a cottage-like cafe that serves up large plates of gourmet American classics loved by health-conscious locals, with breakfast items served until 5pm, plus salads, wraps, paninis, and more. It's a popular brunch spot and you should expect to wait in a long, curvy line around the large, sun-drenched patio – packed with hipsters during peak morning hours – drinking homemade iced tea and lemonade poured for guests waiting in line. You'll probably have to park a block or two away in a municipal car park and pay for a couple of hours, but that's no big deal. Moreover, Los Feliz is

a great place to walk off that big fat brunch you've just consumed; there are a few cool retro-style independent shops to explore, similar in some ways to Silver Lake.

Be sure to sample some of the Alcove's very own chocolate bars – mimosa, red velvet, and salted caramel are just a few flavors – and one of the many tempting baked goods on offer in the pastry window. The adjacent **Big Bar at Alcove** offers hand-crafted cocktails, craft beers, and fine wines alongside reinvented upscale bar food if you're here a bit later in the day. Also check the website for upcoming events such as live music and outdoor screenings.

The Alcove; 1929 Hillhurst Avenue; tel: 323 644-0100; www.alcovecafe.com; map D2

Spend a day inside the Griffith Observatory and watch the breathtaking sunset in the evening

This is a must, that's all there is to it. **The Griffith Observatory** offers the best view of the Los Angeles basin you can possibly get, especially at night. It commands a view of the entire Los Angeles Basin, including Downtown Los Angeles to the southeast, Hollywood to the south, and the Pacific Ocean to the southwest. **Griffith Park** is one of the largest urban parks in the United States and the second-biggest in California; its rugged landscapes and trails make it hugely popular for hikes, including to the Hollywood sign (see page 142).

However, the observatory itself also offers a whole host of attractions and an extensive array of space and science-related displays; you can look through telescopes, explore exhibits, and see live shows. There's always a

mix of both temporary exhibitions that change through the year and permanent ones.

You can spend the day exploring and even have lunch sitting outside in the sunshine, as there's a pretty good restaurant here (the **Café at the End of the Universe**, by Wolfgang Puck). Then get a good spot and watch the sun set to the west. The transition from day to night takes a little while, but it's worth every minute. All you need to do is relax and gaze in wonder as the

On-screen moments

Griffith Observatory has appeared in a number of movies, notably at the beginning of *Terminator* (1984) and in the knife fight in *Rebel Without a Cause* (1955), while a recent showstopper was in the hit musical, *La La Land* (2016), in which Ryan Gosling and Emma Stone have a romantic date roaming (and dancing in) the building.

reds, yellows, and oranges almost make it look like the sky is on fire and as the millions of lights start to come on in the streets below. Like a giant illuminated lattice, they stretch out, extending in every direction to the horizon. Tiny, bright clusters of color seem to shimmer in a big, black ocean, made dark by the night sky above.

Admission to the museum is free, but it's only respectful to leave a donation toward its upkeep. The drive up Mount Hollywood to reach the observatory is along some quite narrow, winding roads, and parking up at the top can be a bit of a nightmare, especially the closer to you get to sunset. Cars can be parked along the side of the road; where there's room they are squeezed into every available space. So maybe brush up on your parallel parking before you attempt this.

Griffith Observatory; 2800 East Observatory Road; tel: 213-473-0800; http://griffithobservatory.org; map C2

Catch a game at Dodger Stadium

This is a must-see on a visit to Los Angeles, providing you visit during the baseball season. Located towards the east end of the Los Angeles basin and east of Downtown, **Dodger Stadium** is a monument to the halcyon days of baseball, with its classic architecture. It's currently the oldest ballpark in MLB (Major League Baseball) west of the Mississippi River, and third-oldest overall, after Fenway Park in Boston and Wrigley Field in Chicago and is the largest MLB stadium by seat capacity. The **LA Dodgers** began, once upon a time, as the Brooklyn Dodgers, but like a few teams in the middle of last century, they migrated west and moved to Los Angeles in 1957.

A baseball game is pretty much a full day out, especially when you factor in the driving to get there. It is accessible by public transport, but public transport hasn't really caught on in LA, so we wouldn't advise it. The car park at Dodger Stadium is the size of a small European country. It's even worth getting to the stadium early and driving up to nearby **Chavez Ridge** in Echo Park: the view over the stadium and Downtown is quite spectacular. There's no shortage of food or drink for lunch or dinner, from a wide range of hot dogs to barbecue wings to replica batter's helmets filled with nachos. There's even a variety of healthy and vegetarian options including sandwiches, sushi, salads, and vegetarian hotdogs.

Much like Angel Stadium in Anaheim (see page 155) tickets to a game will vary greatly in price, depending on where you want to sit and who the game is against. A game of baseball will typically last about three hours and locals like to make a whole evening of it. Sections 11 to 25 are great to catch a potential foul ball but if you fancy your chances of catching a home run, you need to aim for sections 301 to 314 in the left outfield pavilion or right outfield pavilion.

Dodger Stadium; 1000 Vin Scully Avenue; tel: 866-363-4377; http://losangeles. dodgers.mlb.com/la/ballpark; map E1

Enjoy a drink at The Dresden Restaurant

Back in the mid 1990s, there was a big 'swing' revival in Los Angeles and Los Feliz was very much at its center. The superior smash comedy *Swingers* (1996) tapped into this and many of the locations seen in the movie were around Los Feliz, including Jon Favreau's apartment (5874 Franklin Ave), the Los Feliz Golf Club – which is a great fun 9-hole 'pitch and putt'– and **The Dresden Restaurant**.

Something of a Hollywood landmark, this modest looking building is a throwback restaurant and lounge bar that offers classic continental food and live music. The menu includes seafood, prime rib, roast rack of lamb and the mouth-watering Chateaubriand and it's all moderately priced There's live entertainment just about every night of the week and you can even see Marty and Elayne, lounge legends who feature in *Swingers*, every Tuesday through Saturday from 9pm to 1.15am. The eagle-eyed among you might also recognize The Dresden from *That Thing You Do!* (1996) where it also made an appearance.

Sadly, The Derby nightclub, which was one of the venues in Los Feliz that frequently held swing nights, has permanently closed down and the popularity of swing music and 1940s culture has once again disappeared back into the void, waiting patiently for the day it becomes trendy once again. In the meantime though, The Dresden does have a live swing band playing, every once in a while. If swing is your thing though, check out http://swingdance.la for all the events happening in Los Angeles at the time of your visit. You can also find out where to take lessons if you're just getting started. There's good parking around The Dresden and the surrounding area is nice – and perfectly safe – to take an after-dinner stroll in.

The Dresden Restaurant; 1760 N Vermont Avenue; tel: 323-665-4294; www.the dresden.com; map D2

Explore the Eagle Rock neighborhood

Bordered by the city of Glendale to the north and west, **Eagle Rock** is named after a large rock outcropping, resembling an eagle with its wings outstretched. The unusual rock formation is located at the north-east corner of the suburb and you can see it as you whizz past on the Ventura Freeway. But the best view is from Alatorre-Eagle Rock View Park on Scholl Canyon Road. If you are whizzing past on the freeway, just take exit 11, or alternatively cruise up Colorado Boulevard (much nicer) and take N Figueroa Street and head north, under the freeway. It's definitely worth a snap or two.

The area was originally part of the Rancho San Rafael under Spanish and Mexican governorship; today it's an ethnically diverse, relatively high-income and very scenic neighborhood, with lots of interesting, independently-owned little stores, much like Silver Lake and Loz Feliz. Notable residents in the past have included John Steinbeck, Dalton Trumbo, and Marlon Brando.

Eagle Rock is also home to several historic homes, many of which have architectural significance. You can find examples of buildings created in the Crafts-

man, Georgian, Streamline Moderne, Art Deco, and Mission Revival styles. And it's also a favourite location for movie directors. Parts of *Top Gun* (1986) were filmed here, as were TV shows like *Agents of SHIELD* (2013), *NCIS* (2003), and *Arrested Development* (2003). But perhaps most importantly, the diner scene at the beginning of *Reservoir Dogs* (1992) was filmed

here. Today, **Pat & Lorraine's Coffee Shop** is a typical breakfast joint filled every morning by Eagle Rock regulars. Hanging on the walls of the diner, among faded landscapes and still lifes, antique Mexican dolls, and sports portraits from nearby Occidental College is a *Reservoir Dogs* poster and a photograph from the memorable opening scene.

Highland Park streets and alleyways near the warehouse were used for montages of the film's robbery aftermath and the title sequence where the cast walks in slow motion to *Little Green Bag* was shot at a bowling alley just south of Pat & Lorraine's on Eagle Rock Boulevard.

Pat & Lorraine's Coffee Shop; 4720 Eagle Rock Boulevard; tel: 323 257-7926; map E2

141

Hike up to the Hollywood sign and gaze out over the Los Angeles basin

Originally, when it was first built in 1923, the **Hollywood sign** (map C2) read HOLLYWOODLAND and was an advertisement for a local real estate development. It generated a lot of attention and was left standing. However, over the course of more than half a century, the sign, designed to stand for only 18 months, sustained extensive damage and deterioration. For instance, during the early 1940s, the sign's official caretaker Albert Kothe was driving while inebriated and lost control of his vehicle near the top of **Mount Lee**. While he was not injured, his 1928 Ford Model was destroyed along with the letter H that it crashed into.

A public campaign in 1978 was started and nine celebrity donors, including Hugh Hefner, Alice Cooper, and Warner Brothers Records each gave $27,777.77 each, which totaled $250,000, to fund replacement letters. Today, the sign is 45 feet tall, 350 feet long and each letter is made from durable aluminium. You can't actually get too close to the sign, what you have to do is walk the length of Mount Lee to the very end, which goes in a loop of sorts, and that will position you above and behind the sign.

There are a number of different ways to get to the sign, but they all involve quite a lot of walking as **Mount Lee Drive** is closed to public traffic. There are three trails, the **Mt. Hollywood Trail**, the **Canyon Drive Trail**, and the **Cahuenga Peak Trail**; each one has a different starting point and varies in length. The Mt. Hollywood trail starts in Griffith Park, while the Canyon Drive Trail also starts in Griffith Park but goes past Bronson Caves, home of the Batcave, where the Batmobile used to appear and thunder down the road from in the 1960s Adam West *Batman* TV series. Finally, the Cahuenga Peak Hike on the Aileen Getty Ridge Trail starts from the Hugh Hefner Overlook.

It's a great day out of the weather's nice, but be sure to wear light clothing and proper walking shoes, bring water, and apply generous amounts of sun cream.

Wander and hang out in one of Silver Lake's many coffee shops

Silver Lake is a scenic suburb of Los Angeles and while it doesn't have the obvious wealth that Los Feliz does, it's very much a hipster environment that has undergone some gentrification. The indie rock music scene is particularly prominent in this neighborhood and comparisons are often drawn between Silver Lake and New York City's Williamsburg district. As a result, it is sometimes referred to as the 'Williamsburg of the West.'

It was built around what was then a city reservoir, which gives the district its name. The 'silver' in Silver Lake is not because of the water's color, but named for a local politician who helped create the reservoir. Sunset Boulevard runs through the area at the south end and along here you'll find many independently-owned book stores, second-hand clothing stores and record markets, selling sought-after vintage books and vinyl. There are also many more tucked away on the smaller streets too.

Silver Lake is not a particularly big suburb of Los Angeles and many of the coffee shops are situated along Sunset Boulevard and north along Hollywood Boulevard and Hillhurst Avenue. **Intelligentsia Coffee** is a popular choice, as is **Silverlake Coffee**. The former describes itself as a high-end coffee bar serving daily roasted brews in an industrial-chic setting and the latter as an easygoing java joint with free Wi-Fi, light fare, and smoothies, plus a patio and free parking. Every coffee shop in Los Angeles should offer free Wi-Fi, but not every one will offer free parking.

Intelligentsia Coffee; 3922 Sunset Boulevard; tel: 323-663-6173, http://intelligentsiacoffee.com; map D1
Silverlake Coffee; 2388 Glendale Boulevard; tel: 323-913-0388; map D2

Seize the chance to see some space history at JPL

If you're a space buff in any way, shape or form, this is an absolute must. The **Jet Propulsion Laboratory** is a vital element in NASA's research and development program, as any astro-enthusiast will tell you. In the late 1930s, a group of Caltech graduate students were booted off campus after blowing up part of their building during a rocket test gone awry. They continued their experiments and after some success – and proving they could do it without killing themselves – they were given a sizeable grant and moved to a different location. This ultimately became the Jet Propulsion Laboratory and now they have a space program there. Research and engineering under-taken at JPL has given us the Mariner program, Voyager, Pathfinder, and the Spitzer Space Telescope to name just a few.

It's not easy to get on a JPL tour. For starters, they only run them a few times per year and tickets sell like hot cakes, so you'll need to check the JPL website to see when the next tour is being organized. Bear in mind, it could be as much as three or four months away. But, if you do get on a tour, it's well worth it. You'll see inside one of the most significant scientific installations that has contributed to almost every single flight into space in some way. All tours include a presentation, which provides an overview of the laboratory's activities and accomplishments and you can visit the Von Karman Visitor Center, the Space Flight Operations Facility, and the Spacecraft Assembly Facility.

There is also very strict security. It is required that you bring a current, government-issued ID. If you are a US citizen, a driver's license is acceptable. All non-US citizens must bring their passport.

Jet Propulsion Laboratory; 4800 Oak Grove Drive, Pasadena; tel: 818-354-9314; www.jpl.nasa.gov; map F4

Take a gentle stroll around Silver Lake

Silver Lake offers plenty of excuses to get out of your car and explore on foot and one such opportunity is a gentle walk around the **reservoir** (map D2) that gave this neighborhood its name. The neighborhood – and lower lake – was named after the Water Board Commissioner Herman Silver, who was instrumental in the creation of the reservoir. It's composed of two basins: the southern one is named Silver Lake and the northern, smaller one is named Ivanhoe, after the original name for the area, Ivanhoe Canyon. Exactly why it was named after the 1819 Sir Walter Scott novel, no one seems to know.

The reservoir is the focal point of the local community and has evolved as a recreational resource with several popular facilities, including the **Silver Lake Recreation Center** and the adjacent **city park,** which includes a basketball court on the south side, the Silver Lake walking path that circumnavigates the reservoirs (3.62 km/2.25 miles) and the Silver Lake Meadow, modeled after New York's Central Park Sheep Meadow. Its 776 million gallons (3,517 litres) are pumped from the ground beneath Griffith Park's Crystal Springs.

It's a tight community with a sleepy feel to it. There are some lovely houses over the lake as it's also quite an affluent suburb. As a prominent hipster hangout, you will doubtless see lots of runners around the lakes throughout the day and probably one or two people doing yoga.

There were plans to turn the **Ivanhoe Reservoir** into a dedicated recreational beach and swimming area, but these have yet to come to fruition. From time to time they are both drained because of a bromate build up. As a solution to this, they are also sometimes filled with 'bird balls,' over three million of them, to shade the water and prevent a chemical reaction triggered by sunlight that forms bromate. Thankfully though, this doesn't happen too often and the view is largely unspoiled.

LONG BEACH AND ORANGE COUNTY

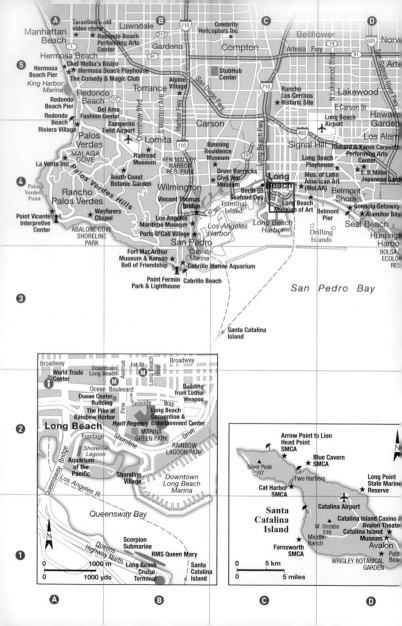

Grid references (top map):

- A
- B
- C
- D

5
Manhattan Beach
Hermosa Beach
Tarantino's old video store
★ Redondo Beach Performing Arts Center
Lawndale
Gardena
Celebrity Helicopters Inc
Bellflower
Norw
Hermosa Beach Pier
★ Chef Melba's Bistro
★ Hermosa Beach Playhouse
The Comedy & Magic Club
King Harbor Marina
Alpine Village
StubHub Center
Compton
Artesia Fwy
Rancho Los Cerritos Historic Site
Lakewood
E Carson St
Long Beach Airport
Hawaii Garden

Redondo Beach Pier
Redondo Beach
Riviera Village
Del Amo Fashion Center
Zamperini Field Airport
Torrance
Crenshaw Blvd
N Western Ave
Harbor Fwy
Carson
San Diego Fwy
Banning Residence Museum
Long Beach
Long Beach Airport
Signal Hill
Los Alam

4
Palos Verdes
La Venta Inn
MALAGA COVE
South Coast Botanic Garden
Railroad Museum
KEN MALLOY HARBOR REG PARK
Lomita
Wilmington
Civil War Museum
Drum Barracks
Vincent Thomas Bridge
Berth 55 Seafood Deli
Terminal Island
Long Beach Museum of Art
Mus. of Latin American Art (MoLAA)
Belmont Shore
Richard & Karen Carpenter Performing Arts Center
E. B. Miller Japanese Gard
Gondola Getaway
Alamitos Bay
Seal Beach

Palos Verdes Point
Rancho Palos Verdes
Palos Verdes Hills
Wayfarers Chapel
Point Vicente Interpretive Center
ABALONE COVE SHORELINE PARK
Los Angeles Maritime Museum
Ports O'Call Village
San Pedro
Cabrillo Marina
Los Angeles Harbor
Long Beach Harbor
Belmont Pier
Drilling Islands
Hunting Harbo
BOLSA ECOLO RES

Fort MacArthur Museum & Korean Bell of Friendship
Point Fermin Park & Lighthouse
Cabrillo Marine Aquarium
Cabrillo Beach

3
San Pedro Bay

Santa Catalina Island

Lower-left map (Long Beach inset):

2
Long Beach
World Trade Center
Broadway
Downtown Long Beach
1st St
Broadway
Avenue
Long Beach Blvd
M
Building from Lethal Weapon
Ocean Center Building
Ocean Boulevard
The Pike at Rainbow Harbor
Seaside Way
Pine
Hyatt Regency
Long Beach Convention & Entertainment Center
Frontage
Shoreline
MARINA GREEN PARK
Drive
RAINBOW LAGOON PARK
Queensway Bridge
Los Angeles R.
Shoreline Lagoon
Aquarium of the Pacific
Shoreline Village
Downtown Long Beach Marina

1
Queensway Bay
Queens Highway North
Scorpion Submarine
RMS Queen Mary
Long Beach Cruise Terminal
Santa Catalina Island

0   1000 m
0   1000 yds

N

- A
- B

Lower-right map (Santa Catalina Island inset):

Arrow Point to Lion Head Point SMCA
Silver Peak 507
Two Harbors
Blue Cavern SMCA
Long Point State Marine Reserve
Cat Harbor SMCA
Santa Catalina Island
M. Orizaba 639 Middle Ranch
Catalina Airport
Catalina Island Casino
Avalon Theatre
Catalina Island Museum
Avalon
Farnsworth SMCA
WRIGLEY BOTANICAL GARDEN
Pebt Bea

0   5 km
0   5 miles

N

- C
- D

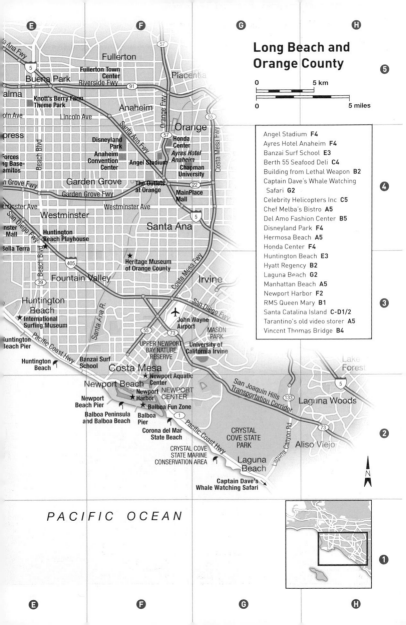

Long Beach and Orange County

0	5 km
0	5 miles

Angel Stadium **F4**
Ayres Hotel Anaheim **F4**
Banzai Surf School **E3**
Berth 55 Seafood Deli **C4**
Building from Lethal Weapon **B2**
Captain Dave's Whale Watching Safari **G2**
Celebrity Helicopters Inc **C5**
Chef Melba's Bistro **A5**
Del Amo Fashion Center **B5**
Disneyland Park **F4**
Hermosa Beach **A5**
Honda Center **F4**
Huntington Beach **E3**
Hyatt Regency **B2**
Laguna Beach **G2**
Manhattan Beach **A5**
Newport Harbor **F2**
RMS Queen Mary **B1**
Santa Catalina Island **C-D1/2**
Tarantino's old video storer **A5**
Vincent Thomas Bridge **B4**

Explore Hermosa and Manhattan Beach, where the sand seems to go on forever

North of Long Beach and located just the other side of the Palos Verdes peninsula, lies a long stretch of beach. Going south to north, skip Redondo and go straight to **Hermosa** (map A5) and **Manhattan Beach** (map A5). Not only are the beaches themselves enormous, but the surrounding neighborhood is well worth a wander around. There's a bohemian vibe here very similar to Venice Beach and while it's got a little commercial in recent years, with more stores selling souvenirs aimed at tourists, there are still a lot of good coffee shops, bars, and restaurants tucked away on side streets.

It's worth dedicating a whole day to gently wandering around this area. Parking might prove a problem, but the best thing to do is leave your car on one of the bigger dedicated sites and pay the all day charge, so you don't have to worry about rushing back to re-fill the meter.

The beachfront walk is popular with walkers, joggers, rollerbladers, and bikers alike and both beaches host professional and amateur volleyball tournaments, festivals, and concerts throughout the year.

There's a wide variety of bars and restaurants, from cheap eats to something a little more upmarket and an equally wide choice of cuisines. **Chef Melba's Bistro** is always very popular and once you've got a table and tried the food, you'll understand why.

Chef Melba's Bistro; 1501 Hermosa Avenue; tel: 310-376-2084; http://chef melbasbistro.com; map A5

Famous faces

This is also the old stomping ground of Quentin Tarantino; the video store (map A5) that he used to work in while he wrote *Reservoir Dogs* (1991) is no longer there, for obvious reasons, but the location is 1822 North Sepulveda Boulevard. The shopping mall, **Del Amo Fashion Center** is also not too far from here (3525 W Carson St; www.simon.com/mall/del-amo-fashion-center; map B5) and along with being where much of *Jackie Brown* was filmed, it's also a popular filming location for many movies and TV programs, from *Malcolm in the Middle* (2000) to *Bad Santa* (2003).

Visit the *Queen Mary*, once the pride of Cunard's cross-Atlantic fleet

An unusual example of British maritime history lies moored in the harbor at Long Beach, the **RMS Queen Mary**. Once the flagship of the Cunard Line, she sailed primarily on the North Atlantic Ocean from 1936 to 1967 between Southampton and New York and even captured the Blue Riband on her maiden voyage on 27 May 1936.

This awesome, 81,961-ton (74,353,768 kg) transatlantic liner has been moored at Long Beach since 1983, where she has served as a tourist attraction, hotel, museum, and event location. Since then she has been bought and sold a number of times, operated as a Hyatt hotel and has even been owned by Disney, who once planned to incorporate her into a huge resort on the adjacent docks called DisneySea, a park themed around the world's oceans. Today however, she is owned by Urban Commons, a real estate company that has announced plans to extensively renovate the liner in 2017–8 and to redevelop the adjacent 45 acres of land. The new development will include a boutique hotel, restaurants, a marina, an amphitheatre, jogging trails, bike paths, and possibly a huge Ferris wheel, all at a cost of up to $250 million (£194 million).

In the meantime, until that's completed, there's still a ton of things you can do onboard, including a very cool tour around the ship late at night. At Halloween, the moored ship's nether parts, including its creepy empty pool, are opened up for ghost-hunting tours and killer mazes. Have a few drinks in the bar and then stumble around hunting the spirits of dead passengers. The ship was even ranked as 'one of the top 10 most haunted places in America' by Time Magazine in 2008.

In particular, Cabin B340 is apparently haunted by the spirit of a person who was murdered there. Spookily, while many hauntings are reported to be the ghosts of drowning victims, the ship's logs do not record any instances to support this.

RMS Queen Mary; 1126 Queens Highway; tel: 877-342-0738; www.queenmary.com; map B1

Get a bird's eye view of Long Beach and cruise over the Vincent Thomas Bridge

Long Beach is not an area that instantly springs to mind when you think of must-see places in Los Angeles, but it is vastly underrated. Many might think of it as just being a base for industry, and while there are significantly-sized dock facilities there, providing a vital link between the US and the Far East, there's also much more. Some places are worth exploring and other sights are just worth a drive-by so you can say you've seen them.

The **Vincent Thomas Bridge** (map B4) is the fourth-longest suspension bridge in California (unsurprisingly, San Francisco's Golden Gate Bridger is first) at 1,500ft (457 meters), crossing the Los Angeles Harbor and linking San Pedro with Terminal Island. The first welded (not riveted) suspension bridge in

Long Beach on location

Long Beach is frequently used for scenes in movies. More often than not, because traffic can be redirected relatively easily without upsetting an entire neighbourhood or blocking a freeway, it's used for car chase scenes. The car chase in *Fletch* (1985) jumps from Wiltshire Boulevard to Long Beach in the blink of an eye. The mafia funeral scene from *The Last Action Hero* (1993) was filmed on the roof of the Hyatt Regency and the circular apartment building seen at the beginning of *Lethal Weapon* (1987) is at 700 E Ocean Boulevard, plus the entire boat chase sequence in *Face/Off* (1997) was filmed in the harbor. The beginning of *The Usual Suspects* (1995) is also set in Long Beach's harbor. The Vincent Thomas Bridge itself pops up in several movies from *Lethal Weapon 2* (1989) to both the original *Gone in 60 Seconds* (1974) and the *Gone in 60 Seconds* remake (2000), where Nicholas Cage jumps a Shelby Mustang GT500 over a roadblock on the bridge.

the US, it opened in 1963 and was named for Californian politician Vincent Thomas of San Pedro, who had been a champion of its construction and saw it as the biggest success of his career. It's the only suspension bridge in the world supported entirely on piles.

As you'll find from time to time exploring Los Angeles, celebrity deaths often garner as much interest as celebrity lifestyles and the Vincent Thomas Bridge is no exception; it was in the news in 2012 when film director Tony Scott committed suicide by jumping from it.

It doesn't take long to drive over the bridge and it's easily added to a pre-planned route that takes in this part of Long Beach. The view of the harbor underneath you and the surrounding area is quite impressive, but the traffic lanes are quite narrow, so be sure to get someone else to take the photographs as concentration on the road is essential.

Soak up the sun at Laguna and Huntington Beach

Two of the most popular water-facing locales in Orange County are Laguna and Huntington beaches and their corresponding neighborhoods. The former is surrounded by an area with much more greenery and natural beauty and consequently offers great places to hike and explore on foot. The latter is a little louder, with a thriving surf scene and some great bars and restaurants. If you venture inland a little from **Laguna Beach** (map G2) you can visit the beautiful little town of San Juan Capistrano, where the old Spanish Mission still stands. There are some great restaurants here, all locally-owned and offering locally caught or grown food.

From **Newport Harbor** (map F2) you can take any one of a number of boat excursions where, hopefully, you'll see the telltale blows and tail slaps that indicate that humpback, minke, grey, finback, or giant blue whales are near. You could also arrange a fishing trip with any one of a number of vendors, but these will vary during the year. The best thing to do if this floats your boat, is to check online and see what's available at a time of your choice. Alternatively, there are some great golf courses in the area.

Huntington beach (map E3) has a more vibrant pulse to it. During the summer, big events like the Sundown EDM music festival draw huge crowds that dance through the night on the sand. Usually in the last week of July, the best surfers in the world convene on Huntington Beach for a full week of competition; the event also draws big crowds from other sports like BMX and skateboarding. There's a big microbrewery scene here and many of the bars offer local, home-grown flavours. Get a group together, play some volleyball on the beach and later, as the sun starts to set, use one of the many specially designated fire pits on the beach and barbecue dinner.

Watch the notorious Anaheim Ducks play

Every now and again, a fictional product or brand from a movie is made into a product or brand in real life; like Bubba Gump Shrimp from *Forest Gump* (1994). In 1992 Emilio Estevez and Joshua Jackson starred in a movie called *The Mighty Ducks*, which was a sports comedy about a lacklustre kids' ice hockey team that get their act together and ultimately win the championship. A year later, Disney entered a new team in the NHL and named them the **Mighty Ducks** and they have become a force to be reckoned with. They were sold to a private owner in 2005, but since their unusual beginnings they have won the Pacific Division six times, the Western Conference championship twice and the coveted Stanley Cup in the 2006/07 season. They make the playoffs pretty much every year and are an exciting, hard-hitting team to watch.

The Ducks, as they're now known, play in Anaheim at the **Honda Center**. The ice hockey season starts in October and runs through to June, with the regular season ending in April, when the playoffs – or postseason – games begin. NHL (National Hockey League) consists of three 20-minute periods played at breakneck speed, with

a 20-minute gap in-between each period. Americans love to make a whole night out of a sports game, be it baseball, American Football (NFL), or ice hockey. Crowds really get behind their teams and if you're lucky, you'll be surrounded by dedicated supporters of the local team who will teach you the chants and slogans you need to shout, especially if a fight breaks out on the ice, at which point you'll see the stadium descend into chaos.

Honda Center; 2695 East Katella Avenue; http://honda.centeranaheim.com; map F4

Get onto the field with the Los Angeles Angels

Baseball is probably America's national sport. American Football, or NFL, always whips up public interest and simultaneously unites and divides the nation, but the NFL season is short – just six months from start to finish, whereas baseball seems to run almost all year round.

Los Angeles has two teams, the **Dodgers** (see page 138) and the **Angels**. However, because they're based in Anaheim, they're sometimes referred to as the Anaheim Angels, or even the Los Angeles Angels of Anaheim. (Something you might struggle to fit on a cap.) Regardless, they're a fun team to watch and usually mill about somewhere in the middle of the league. They play at **Angel Stadium** (2000 Gene Autry Way), which is very easy to get to and offers plenty of

parking. There are a number of good hotels within walking distance, from mid-range to high-end. The **Ayres Hotel Anaheim** (2550 E Katella Ave) is one, and if there are no big business conferences or exhibitions on, you can sometimes get a cheaper rate as they're eager to fill the rooms.

A game of baseball will typically last about three hours. Again,

Americans like to make a whole evening of it. But there's plenty of food and beer available in the stadium. Tickets to a game will vary greatly in price, depending on where you want to sit and who the game is against. A game against the New York Yankees, for example, will probably inflate the tickets prices a bit as opposed to a game against say, the Toronto Blue Jays. If money is no object, the seats behind the home plate are considered the best, if you can get them. Failing that, the two sections either side of the home plate are good as that's where fans hope to catch a foul ball. Different sites will have different seating charts, but it's typically areas 109 to 113 and 123 to 127.

Alternatively, if you're feeling lucky, seats at the far end are also popular, on the off chance that you might catch a home-run ball. While the fence line is an attractive option, your best shot at catching one of those out-of-the-park homers is situating yourself in sections 236, 240, 257, or 260. There's a good guide at https://seatgeek.com/home-run that's pretty helpful.

Angel Stadium; 2000 Gene Autry Way; http://losangeles.angels.mlb.com/ana/ballpark; map F4

Chow down where the locals eat at the back-to-basics Berth 55 Seafood Deli

Another reason to drive all the way to Long Beach is to eat at the back-to-basics **Berth 55**, where you can buy live lobster, grilled salmon, and/or fresh Alaskan king crab legs and eat them while looking at the looming shipping cranes of the city's largest economic engine. Head towards Pico Avenue (definitely not to be mistaken with Pico Boulevard), pull into the parking lot of Berth 55 Fish Market and Seafood Deli, saunter into the corrugated metal shack structure, order whatever looks good from the chilled glass cabinets, and sit on the bright red picnic tables outside until your number is called.

You will be dining off a paper plate, but all the better, because this is satisfying, essential cooking that seems appropriate to eat with your hands. Crack open buttery, steamed crabs legs, tuck into shrimp skewers or fresh scallops, or come in the winter for a deeply warming sourdough bowl of clam chowder.

Chances are you'll be the only non-local there and you'll probably see an array of the types that populate this industrial epicenter of Southern California, from truck drivers to dirty dungaree-wearing dockworkers to fishermen who charter boats from the harbor. All of these people probably depend on Long Beach in one way or another for their livelihood. This isn't the kind of place where anyone will ask if everything is all right with your meal and chances are the table will still have a pile of plates from the last person who sat there – this is a no-frills eatery that primarily serves the blue-collar workers and residents of Long Beach and it has more personality than many of the high-end places that charge ten times as much. Be sure to leave a nice tip and contribute in a small way to its survival.

Berth 55; 555 Pico Avenue; Long Beach; tel: 562-435-8366; www.berth55seafood. com; map C4

Spend a day at the iconic Disneyland Park

Disneyland, now called **Disneyland Park**, was the first of two enormous theme parks branded with that instantly recognizable icon of black, round mouse ears. The other of course is Disney World in Orlando, Florida. This one however, was the only one built under the direct supervision of Mr Walt Disney himself. Having visited amusement parks with his daughters, he developed the concept and the park was finally opened in July 1955.

Today, thousands visit the park every day, which adds up to tens of millions every year. Every few years modifications are made, with an outdated ride being replaced or a new one added, and since Disney's multi-billion dollar acquisition of two of cinema's biggest franchises, Marvel and Star Wars, Disneyland Park is only going to get bigger. In fact, **Star Wars Land** opens in 2019 and early images of its construction are already circulating online. It's probably safe to say it's going to be pretty spectacular once completed.

In the meantime however, there are literally hundreds of rides, experiences, and attractions to enjoy. It's definitely worth having a look at the website to see the latest news and events. Some of the popular rides include Big Thunder Mountain Railroad, Space Mountain, Indiana Jones Adventure, and Gadget's Go Coaster. There are restaurants and bars inside, more gift shops that you can count and attractions for kids (and adults) of all ages.

All this fun does come at a price. The cost of a one-day pass varies depending on the time of year and a two-day pass starts at $100 (£77). This doesn't include parking, naturally, which starts at $20 (£15) per day. Unfortunately, a car is really the best way to get there and after a day on your feet (be sure to wear comfortable shoes), you will be glad you took it.

Disneyland Park; Disneyland Drive; tel: 714-781-4565; https://disneyland.disney.go.com; map F4

Have a swell time and take a surf lesson at Huntington Beach

If you've timed your visit to coincide with the surfing season, then it would be rude not to at least take a lesson and try it once, assuming of course that you're not already an avid surfer. And there's no better place to head to than **Huntington Beach**, the official Surf City USA. Thanks to the beach's consistent, year-round swell and the area's resultant surf culture, this is the place to really discover California's boardie paradise. The 10-mile (16km) coastline offers five distinct beaches, all of which are good for different surf levels, so you can work your way up from a calm paddle in smoother waters to shredding the big waves by the pier. Feel free to bring your own board, but it's as easy to rent one, or book a lesson from one of the trusted surf schools here.

There's quite a few to choose from and all come highly recommended, but the **Banzai Surf School** is probably one of the best. Lessons start at $85 per person for one hour or you can take a two-hour lesson for $149. If you are looking to learn to surf, this is their most popular lesson and includes both surfboard and wetsuit hire, a 20 minute-briefing on safety and a land demonstration, followed by 90 minutes or more in the water. Or you can take a private lesson, ideal for children and older people (or 'silver surfers'), or simply anyone looking to improve.

If you're really determined to learn to surf, they even offer week-long, summer surf camps, from $390 per person. There are occasional shark sightings in the waters off Orange County, but the water around Huntington Beach is vigorously patrolled by the Coast Guard and lifeguards, by air and by boat, and there has never been an incident here. Statistically speaking you probably have a higher chance of being hit by a bus than attacked by a shark.

Banzai Surf School; 22355 Pacific Coast Highway; tel: 714 813-2880; http://banzai surfschool.com; map E3

Go whale spotting with Captain Dave and his crew

Regardless of what time of year you visit, you're pretty much guaranteed to see something, almost certainly dolphins, minke whales, and humpback whales as they're about all year round, but if you're looking for blue or finback whales, you need to ship out in September. A trip with Captain Dave on a whale-watching safari is usually a two and a half hour trip and once in a while killer whales, Bryde's whales, sei whales, sperm whales, and pilot whales are spotted. Forget aquariums – this is the best and only way to see oceanic wildlife, in its natural environment, swimming freely and uncontained.

Captain Dave's **Whale Watching Safari** is one of the most popular in the area and gets rave reviews. The catamaran also has underwater viewing pods to enable you to see these magnificent animals under the surface; you can listen to dolphins during your whale-watch with an underwater hydrophone, and there are even triple-fudge brownies to munch on along the way. There are a number of different tours and only a certain amount of people are allowed on each boat trip.

Daily tours start at $65 (£50) each for adults, $45 (£34) for children aged 1 to 12 and $20 (£15) if they're under 12 months. It's best to check the website for details nearer the time you're planning to take a tour, as of course factors like the weather can affect them. If you really want to splash out you can hire a boat for a private party. Again, best to call ahead to check availability.

Captain Dave's Whale Watching Safari; 24440 Dana Point Harbor Dr, Dana Point; tel: 949-488-2828; www.dolphinsafari.com; map G2

Gaze in awe upon Los Angeles from the best vantage point – the air

Robin C Petgrave is the chief pilot of **Celebrity Helicopters Inc.** and he offers a multitude of different tours over the city of Los Angeles.

Trips include the Sightseers Dream, starting at $99, which whirls you around the beaches and ports of Los Angeles' south bay (approx. 25-minute flight) and the USA Gateway Tour over San Pedro and the Port of Los Angeles, also $99 and a 15–25 minute flight. The Deluxe Champagne Tour is a light airplane tour that covers all the sites of LA while sipping on champagne. This is a 55-minute flight and will set you back $209. The Hollywood Strip Tour is a helicopter ride around the famous tourist spots such as The Walk of Fame, Hollywood Hills, and Hollywood Strip and is a 15-30 minute flight costing $199. The Beach Cities Tour is a 30-minute helicopter tour of LA's breathtaking coast including Palos Verdes and the South Bay and will cost you $189. The LA Tour takes about 25 minutes and covers a little bit of everything from Downtown to West Hollywood and costs $219. The Celebrity Homes Tour is, according to the website, the most popular and it's not hard to imagine why. This helicopter tour lasts about 35 minutes and costs $219. Or you could witness the illuminated lattice of Los Angeles at night from the air on the Original Night Tour that lasts about 40 minutes and will set you back $269.

Alternatively, you could take in the beaches, the celebrity homes and downtown all in one flight, in the VIP Grand Tour that lasts 55 minutes and costs $319. There's even the option to customize your own tour. A sunset can be requested, but never guaranteed.

Celebrity Helicopters, Inc.; 961 West Alondra Boulevard, Compton; tel: 877-999-2099; www.celebheli.com; map C5

Discover the wildlife, dive sites, and mountains of Santa Catalina Island

Southwest of Los Angeles lie California's Channel Islands, of which **Santa Catalina** (map C2/D1) is the best known. Its main attractions include its wildlife, great dive sites, and Mt Orizaba, its highest peak. To the north lies the resort town of Two Harbors, while to the south, in the city of **Avalon**, palm trees and cabanas line Descanso Beach, which has a charming, vacation feel. Avalon's circular, Art Deco **Catalina Casino** is in fact a cultural center, with a movie theater, ballroom and museum – but no gambling.

A trip here represents a breather from the busyness of the 'mainland,' and Avalon's relaxed vibe is perfect for an easy-going day out, whether you want to partake in some of the many activities on offer, or just enjoy the Mediterranean climate, ocean air, and sunny ambiance. There are plush hotels and soothing spas, and its full of places to eat, drink, shop and explore.

Catalina has had many claimants over the years. It was first settled by Native Americans, while the first Europeans who landed on Catalina claimed it for Spain. As with the rest of the region, claims to the island transferred first to Mexico and then to the US over time. For years, the island was sometimes used as a base for smugglers and gold digging, before William Wrigley Jr – the chewing gum magnate – developed Catalina into a tourist destination in the 1920s.

The best way to get to the island is on the **Catalina Express**, which takes just an hour. There is a year-round service and up to 30 daily departures. Boats depart ports in Long Beach, San Pedro, and Dana Point. Once on the island you can book a tour that takes you further out into the Pacific on a boat with a clear, glass hull or hire some kayaks and paddle out yourself. Alternatively, take a tour that takes you around the island, or you can just explore at your own leisure. Stay for a day or a few days, but be sure to book everything before you travel.

www.catalinaexpress.com

ESSENTIALS

A

AGE RESTRICTIONS

You must be over 21 years of age to drink legally in Los Angeles. Expect to show ID when buying alcohol in bars, clubs, and restaurants.

C

CHILDREN

Los Angeles is very kid-friendly, with an abundance of playgrounds, restaurants that offer children's menus, bathrooms equipped with changing tables for babies, and lots of open space. Most hotels allow children to stay in parents' rooms at no additional charge.

Good internet resources for family travel include www.travelforkids.com, www.takingthekids.com, www.ciaobambino.com, www.kids-world-travel-guide.com, and www.redtri.com.

CLIMATE

Much of Los Angeles has a Mediter-ranean-like climate with warm, dry summers and mild, wet winters.

Spring is warm and sunny (average high in April 71°F/22°C; low 54°F/12°C). During May, June and July, early morning fog may affect the coastal strip. During the summer, average highs soar into the mid-80s (average high in July 82°F/28°C; low 64°F/18°C). Come

October and November, the summer heat is replaced with beautifully mild, sunny days (average high in October 77°F/25°C; low 58°F/15°C).

Winters are mildly cool to warm with the occasional rainstorm in December and January (average high in January 68°F/20°C; low 48°F/9°C).

CLOTHING

The sun shines pretty much every day in Los Angeles, so sunglasses are imperative, especially when you're driving. Layers are the key to surviving in Southern California. During the winter, the temperature can drop a little and it's always amusing to see locals dressed up like they're in the Arctic when, to most other people, it's really not that cold at all. A second layer is usually all that's required during the day – not a winter coat and wool hat.

During the summer, it can get pretty hot, especially inland and away from the ocean, so you'll appreciate light dresses and a few pairs of shorts, or the equivalent, and plenty of t-shirts. Take shoes that are comfortable to drive in and comfortable to walk in. Some of the high-end bars and restaurants will require something a little smarter, so while you won't need a tie, trousers other than jeans and shoes other than trainers will be required. Aside from that, LA is a pretty liberal place, so you can wear whatever you want.

CRIME AND SAFETY

Travelers should exercise common sense, avoiding seedy neighborhoods and being cautious about walking around alone and at night. Avoid parks after dark. Neighborhoods with less safe reputations include the South, parts of Downtown, South Figueroa Corridor, Vernon/Main, and the Fashion District.

CUSTOMS

Adult visitors staying longer than 72 hours may bring the following into the country duty-free: 1 litre of wine or liquor; 100 cigars (non-Cuban), or 3lbs of tobacco, or 200 cigarettes; and gifts valued under $100.

No food (even in cans) or plants are permissible. Visitors may also arrive and depart with up to $10,000 currency without needing to declare it. For the most up-to-date information, refer to the US Customs and Border Protection website (www.cbp.gov).

D

DISABLED TRAVELERS

The city's topography presents challenges to those who have mobility problems, but Los Angeles is relatively 'disabled-friendly.'

Organizations that can provide useful information include the LA Tourism & Convention Board (tel: 323-467-6412; www.discoverlosangeles.com) and the Society for Accessible Travel & Hospitality (SATH; Tel: 212-447-7284; www.sath.org).

E

ELECTRICITY

Electricity in the US is 110 Volts, 60 Hertz AC. Flat-blade, two-pronged plugs are typical, though some points have three-pronged sockets. Most foreign appliances need a transformer and/or plug adapter.

EMBASSIES AND CONSULATES

Australia: Tel: 310-229-2300; www.losangeles.consulate.gov.au
Canada: Tel: 213-346-2700; www.can-am.gc.ca/los-angeles
Ireland: Tel: 714-658-9832; www.dfa.ie
New Zealand: Tel: 310-566-6555; www.mfat.govt.nz
South Africa: Tel: 323-651-0902; www.dirco.gov.za
UK: Tel: 310-789-0031; www.gov.uk
Details for other embassies and consulates can be found in the Yellow Pages.

EMERGENCY NUMBERS

For ambulance, fire, or police, dial 911; if you need to call from a public phone, no coins are needed.

F

FESTIVALS

Check www.discoverlosangeles.com/what-to-do/events for festival and events listings.

H

HEALTH

Drugstores (pharmacies)

Some medicines that are available over the counter at home may require a prescription in the US. Branches of 24-hour Walgreens drugstore include: 8770 W Pico Blvd, tel: 310-275-2117; 1501 Vine St, tel: 310-467-7916. Additional Walgreens branches are open late.

Insurance and hospitals

Health care is private and can be very expensive, especially if you need to be hospitalized. Foreign visitors should always ensure that they have full medical insurance covering their stay before traveling to the US. The following hospitals have 24-hour emergency rooms:

Cedars-Sinai Medical Center
8700 Beverly Blvd., tel: 310-423-3277; www.cedars-sinai.edu
Providence St. Joseph Medical Center
501 S. Buena Vista St., Burbank, tel: 818-843-5111; www.california. providence.org/saint-joseph
Ronald Reagan UCLA Medical Center
757 Westwood Plaza, tel: 310-825-9111; www.uclahealth.org/reagan
UCLA Medical Center, Santa Monica
1250 16th St., Santa Monica, tel: 424-259-6000; www.uclahealth.org/santa-monica

I

INTERNET

Many cafes and some hotels have free or inexpensive Wi-Fi, and public library branches provide free web access (Los Angeles Public Library; Tel: 213-228-7000; www.lapl.org).

L

LGBTQ TRAVELERS

Los Angeles is internationally known as one of the world's most welcoming places for gay and lesbian travelers. The most predominantly gay districts are West Hollywood (aka WeHo), Silver Lake, and Los Feliz. The best source for information is LA's only LGBT free weekly, *The Pride LA* (www.thepridela.com). The LGBT Center (1625 N. Schrader Boulevard; Tel: 323-993-7400; www.lalgbtcenter. org) is a hub for the local LGBT community. Also, check out www.discover losangeles.com/gayla for up-to-the-minute events and guides.

M

MEDIA

The largest regional newspaper is the *Los Angeles Times* (www.latimes. com) and another national daily of the area is the *Orange County Register* (www.ocregister.com). If you can find one, a free weekly called LA Weekly (www.laweekly.com) is excellent. As a result the storage bins that are filled with them every Thursday empty out pretty quick. Many people in Los Angeles read *The New York Times* and treat that as their national daily. TV in Los Angeles is much the same as it is across the US; CNN, Fox, ABC, and NBC are the main news networks.

MONEY

Currency

The dollar ($) is divided into 100 cents (¢). Common coins are the penny (1¢), nickel (5¢), dime (10¢), and quarter (25¢). Common bills are $1, $5, $10, $20, $50, and $100.

Banks and currency exchange

Bank hours are generally Monday to Friday, from about 9am to 5pm. Some open on Saturdays. It's best to change foreign currency at ATMs, airports, and major banks downtown.

ATMs

ATMs are found at banks, some stores and bars, and charge varying usage fees: check also with your bank at home.

Traveler's checks

Though not nearly as common as they once were, banks, stores, restaurants, and hotels generally accept traveler's checks in US dollars.

POLICE

The emergency police number is 911 (no coins needed if calling from a payphone). The non-emergency number for the police is 1-877-ASK-LAPD (1-877-275-5273).

POSTAL SERVICES

Post offices open at 8–9am and close at 5–6pm, Monday through Friday; post offices at 406 E 2nd St (tel: 213-613-0701), 110 S Fairfax Ave (tel: 323-933-2322) and 3707 Hill St (tel: 800-275-8777) are open on Saturday and Sunday.

US Postal Service: Tel: 1-800-ASK-USPS (1-800-275-8777); www.usps. com.

PUBLIC HOLIDAYS IN CALIFORNIA

New Year's Day (Jan 1); Martin Luther King Jr. Day (3rd Monday in January); President's Day (3rd Monday in February), Cesar Chavez Day (March 31); Memorial Day (Last Monday in May); Independence Day (July 4); Labor Day (1st Monday in September); Veterans Day (Nov 11); Thanksgiving Day (4th Thursday in November); day after Thanksgiving (4th Friday in November); and Christmas Day (Dec 25).

S

SMOKING

Smoking laws are strict, and smoking is banned in many public places such as offices, shops, restaurants, bars, parks, playgrounds, and beaches. Many hotels are completely non-smoking and impose heavy fines on violators. The legal smoking age is 21.

T

TAXES

In Los Angeles, a 9 percent sales tax is added to the price of all goods and services. Santa Monica, Culver City, and City of Commerce come in at 9.5 percent. Hotels charge a 14 percent tax that generally will not be included in quoted rates.

TELEPHONES

Local calls are inexpensive; long-distance calls are not. Public phones accept coins and calling cards. The Los Angeles area codes are 310 and 424; the country code is 1. Toll-free numbers begin 1-800, 1-888, 1-877, or 1-866.

Directory enquiries: 411.

US calls outside your area code: 1 + area code + phone number. International calls: 011+ country code + phone number.

Operator: 0 for assistance with local calls; 00 for international calls.

TIME ZONES

Los Angeles is on Pacific Standard Time. PST is three hours behind Eastern Standard Time (New York) and eight hours behind Greenwich Mean Time (London).

TIPPING

Restaurants: 20 percent (even if you were unsatisfied with the service you should tip). Most restaurants add a service charge automatically for parties of six or more.

Taxis: 10–20 percent

Bars: 10–15 percent, or at least $1–2 per drink

Coat check: $1–2 per coat

Door attendants: $1–2 for hailing a cab or bringing in bags

Porters: $1–2 per bag

Valet parking: $5–10

Concierge: $5–10

Maids: $3–5 per day

Hairdressers and salons: 15–20 percent

Tour guides: 15 percent

TOURIST INFORMATION

Visitor Information Center of Los Angeles: 6801 Hollywood Blvd, Tel: 323-467-6412; www.discoverlos angeles.com; Mon–Sat 8am–10pm, Sun 9am–7pm. There's also an information center at Union Station, 800 N. Alameda St; Mon-Sun 9am–5pm. Times may differ on public holidays.

The center's multilingual staff answer travel questions, provide directions and public transportation information, assist with itineraries and make recommendations on dining, sightseeing, and cultural options. Centers also sell tickets to attractions and provide maps and travel guides.

TRANSPORTATION SECURITY ADMINISTRATION

It's worth double checking the TSA website (www.tsa.gov) for the most up to date immigration information. At the time of going to print, it is possible that laptops may be banned from carry on luggage on all international flights to the US.

TRANSPORTATION

A major hub for flights from all over the world, Los Angeles is easily reached by air, while visitors from other parts of the United States can opt to travel by rail or bus. Once here, the city and its outlying areas are comfortably navigable by public transportation.

Getting to Los Angeles

By air

Los Angeles International Airport (LAX; 1 World Way; Tel: 855-463-5252; www.airport-la.com www.lawa.org)

is the major international airport for southwestern California. From Europe, all the major airlines offer non-stop flights or connections via New York, Chicago, or San Francisco. It also receives non-stop, or one-stop, flights from all the principal Pacific airports. Despite being 18 and 12 miles away respectively, downtown Los Angeles and Santa Monica are easy to reach.

Among the modes of transportation available at LAX are an airport bus service, door-to-door shuttle van service, local bus lines, light rail, rental cars, and taxicabs. A free, frequent shuttle bus connects LAX with METRO's Green Line Light Rail. Shuttle service is provided at no charge for passengers making connecting flights between terminal buildings.

The **LAX FlyAway** bus service provides frequent nonstop transportation between LAX and Van Nuys Bus Terminal, Union Station in Downtown Los Angeles and Westwood/UCLA (Tel: 866-435-9529; www.lawa.org/FlyAway).

The **Ontario International Airport** (ONT; 2500 Airport Drive, Ontario; Tel: 909-937-2700; www.flyontario.com) is located 38 miles east of Downtown LA. A great alternative as it serves Anaheim and the greater Orange County and southern California, however there is no direct public transport to Downtown LA, so hiring a car should be considered.

John Wayne International Airport (SNA; 18601 Airport Way, Santa Ana; Tel: 949-252-5200; www.ocair.com) in Santa Ana, Orange County is not far from Disneyland. The Disneyland Resort Express bus stop is located on the Arrival (lower) Level in the Ground Transportation Center. Regional buses and trains are located in Irvine, Santa Ana and Tustin, approximately 10 miles from the airport.

By train

Located in Downtown Los Angeles, Union Station is the largest railroad passenger terminal in the Western United States. **Amtrak** have several routes that run to Union Station (800 North Alameda Street; information line: 800-872-7245; www.amtrak. com). This historic station is also the hub of the **Metrolink** commuter trains, and several **Metro Rail** subway and light rail lines, taxi, and private shuttles serve it as well.

By bus

The **Los Angeles Bus Station** (1716 East 7th St; information line: 1-800-231-2222; www.greyhound.com) is a major hub for the long range Greyhound bus service.

Megabus also runs to Los Angeles Union Station from several Californian locations, including Las Vegas (tel: 877-462-6342; www.us.megabus. com) and **California Shuttle Bus** provides daily bus services between Los Angeles, San Francisco and San Jose (tel: 877-225-0287; www.cashuttle bus.com). **Bolt Bus** also runs buses between Los Angeles and San Jose/ San Francisco. They have stops in Downtown LA and Hollywood (tel: 877-265-8287; www.boltbus.com).

By car

Los Angeles is easy to reach by car. The vast network of highways includes I-5 from San Diego or Sacramento, US Hwy 101 from the north, I-15 from Las Vegas and I-10 from Phoenix. State Highway 1 runs along the coast of California and the western part of San Francisco.

Getting around Los Angeles

For a free traveler information service to help you navigate the entire Los Angeles public transit system, including Muni Lines, Metro Rail, and cycling routes call 511 or look online at www.go511.com); 511 offers assistance with planning trips using public transportation, traffic, and drive-time information.

Buses and metro

There are over 200 metro bus lines and 6 metro rail lines in the Los Angeles area. Detailed information, along with a trip planner, can be found here: www.metro.net (Transit information 323.GO.METRO (323-466-3876) and www.socaltransport.org.

LADOT, the Los Angeles Department of Transportation, www.ladottransit.com operates the city's bus service and connects to the bus systems of surrounding cities and to Metro buses. LADOT also runs the DASH system, the Commuter Express, and the San Pedro Trolley system as well as City Hall and Metrolink shuttles downtown.

DASH provides frequent, inexpensive and convenient bus services in Downtown Los Angeles and in 27 neighbourhoods all across the City of Los Angeles.

Commuter Express makes a limited number of stops, making travel times around the city as short as possible.

Metrolink is a commuter rail system serving five counties in the southern California area. The system is centered at Los Angeles Union Station (tel: 800-371-5465; www.metrolinktrains.com).

For up-to-the-minute information on when the transportation you are waiting for will arrive, visit www.nextmuni.com or www.metro.net/riding/nextrip.

You can download route maps for free online or smartphone users can download the Go Metro app, which includes an interactive map with live departure and arrival times, total trip time and exact fare pricing.

Taxis

Taxis are a convenient but expensive way to get around when the majority of Los Angeles' public transit shuts down around 12.30am. There are about a dozen or so taxicab companies in Los Angeles. Taxi drivers are allowed to drop off passengers in any of the areas, but they can only pick up passengers in their authorized zone. So you will need to call the appropriate cab company, depending on where you want to be picked up.

The website www.taxifarefinder.com provides estimates for taxi fares. You can enter your starting point and destination using street addresses or points of interest (such as airports or tourist destinations). The estimated fare is calculated based on the mileage, approximate time and predetermined rates. So it's not exact, but it will give you an idea of the cost. For the most accurate estimates, you should call each taxi cab company directly and ask for a quote.

Alternatively, you can now get a private car service using smartphone apps like Uber (www.uber.com), Lyft (www.lyft.com) and Sidecar (www.side.cr). An account with these companies must be set up and their app must be downloaded on to your smartphone in order to request ride service.

If money is no object and you just don't want the hassle of driving in LA, you can always hire a car and driver to be at your beck and call and take you everywhere you want to go. If you're traveling alone, it gives you the added bonus of being able to take carpool lanes on the freeway, reducing time in transit for greater distances. If you're traveling with a group or family, it can end up being less expensive than buying individual tours or shuttle fares for everyone in your group. Check out www.avis.com or www.wedriveu.com.

Cycling
Around Los Angeles, there are plenty of paved and designated trails that hug the beach and tour LA's best parks. Cycling along 22-mile Marvin Braude Bike Trail (aka the Strand) is a favorite. Bikes can be rented hourly or for the day, with rates varying by type of bike, but usually $35-80 per day (8 hours). Tour operators: **Bikes and Hikes LA** (tel: 323-796-8555; www.bikesand hikesla.com)

Electric bikes at **Pedal or Not** (tel: 310-917-1111; http://pedalornot.net) **Perrys Beach Rentals** (tel: 310-939-000; www.perryscafe.com) Useful planner: www.ridethecity.com

Driving
Los Angeles is world-famous for its car culture. With many attractions spread out around the city, a car is the most convenient way to explore Los Angeles and its surrounding areas. All major car-rental companies have outlets at Los Angeles International Airport and around the city.

V

VISA INFORMATION
Visit the US Department of State web site (www.travel.state.gov) or Tel: 202-663-1225 for information about visas. Visitors from the UK, Australia, New Zealand, and Ireland qualify for the visa waiver program, and therefore do not need a visa for stays of less than 90 days, as long as they have a valid 10-year machine-readable passport and a return ticket. However, they must apply online for authorization at least 72 hours before traveling at https://esta.cbp.dhs.gov. Citizens of South Africa need a visa. All foreign visitors have their two index fingers scanned and a digital photograph taken at the port of entry. The process takes only 10–15 seconds.

W

WEBSITES
Some helpful sites include:
Official website for L.A. Tourism: www.discoverlosangeles.com (LA Tourism & Convention Board)
City of Los Angeles: www.lacity.org
Official website of the City of Los Angeles Department of Cultural Affairs. www.culturela.org
City of Los Angeles Convention Center www.lacclink.com

INDEX

Experience Los Angeles
Editor: Sarah Clark
Author: Scott Snowden
Update Production: Apa Digital
Head of Production: Rebeka Davies
Picture Editor: Tom Smyth
Cartography: Carte
Photography: 4Corners Images 1, 4/5, 6, 24, 56, 76, 82/83, 98, 102/103, 106/107, 139; Alamy 29, 33, 40, 44, 45, 49, 66, 69, 73, 80/81, 85, 87, 105, 122, 128/129, 140/141, 143, 145, 146; Berth 55 158; Carol M. Highsmith/Library of Congress 91, 111; Cheese Store of Beverly Hills 126; David Dunai/Apa Publications 32, 55, 119, 151, 154, 160; Disney Enterprises, Inc 159; Downtown LA Walking Tours 70; Edmund Vermeulen 134; Eye Ubiquitous/REX/Shutterstock 39; Gareth Simpson 110; Getty Images 28, 30/31, 36/37, 48, 54, 60, 63, 64, 65, 67, 88, 89, 92, 95, 96, 108, 112, 113, 114, 121, 124, 130, 135, 138, 144, 152/153, 155, 156/157, 163; GRAMMY Museum 72; Henry Hargreaves/Nobu Restaurants 38; Innovative Dining Group 86; iStock 21, 46/47, 52/53, 68, 71, 75, 82, 118, 136/137, 150, 162; Jeff Turner 109; Jody Horton 123; Leonardo 97; Los Angeles Philharmonic 93; Mike Johnson/DolphinSafari.com 161; Rhythm Room LA 74; Shutterstock 51, 84, 127, 142; Stahl House 90; SuperStock 35, 61; Sushi Roku 34; Tomoko Spa 125; Venice Ale House 50; Warner Bros. Studio Tour Hollywood 104
Cover: Shutterstock

Distribution
UK, Ireland and Europe
Apa Publications (UK) Ltd;
sales@insightguides.com
United States and Canada
Ingram Publisher Services;
ips@ingramcontent.com
Australia and New Zealand
Woodslane; info@woodslane.com.au

Southeast Asia
Apa Publications (SN) Pte;
singaporeoffice@insightguides.com
Hong Kong, Taiwan and China
Apa Publications (HK) Ltd;
hongkongoffice@insightguides.com
Worldwide
Apa Publications (UK) Ltd;
sales@insightguides.com

Special Sales, Content Licensing and CoPublishing
Insight Guides can be purchased in bulk quantities at discounted prices. We can create special editions, personalised jackets and corporate imprints tailored to your needs.
sales@insightguides.com
www.insightguides.biz

First Edition 2017

Contact us
Every effort has been made to provide accurate information in this publication, but changes are inevitable. The publisher cannot be responsible for any resulting loss, inconvenience or injury. We would appreciate it if readers would call our attention to any errors or outdated information. We also welcome your suggestions; please contact us at:
hello@insightguides.com
www.insightguides.com